THE CASE AGAINST BLACK REPARATION

A Bible Teacher's analysis of the problems faced in seeking to compensate Black Americans for the unpaid labor of their slave ancestors

Wm. L. Banks, D. Min.

Copyright © 2001 by Wm L. Banks, D. Min

All rights reserved. No part of this book shall be reproduced or transmitted in any form or by any means, electronic, mechanical, magnetic, photographic including photocopying, recording or by any information storage and retrieval system, without prior written permission of the publisher. No patent liability is assumed with respect to the use of the information contained herein. Although every precaution has been taken in the preparation of this book, the publisher and author assume no responsibility for errors or omissions. Neither is any liability assumed for damages resulting from the use of the information contained herein.

ISBN 978-0-7414-0800-6

INFINITY PUBLISHING
1094 New DeHaven Street, Suite 100
West Conshohocken, PA 19428-2713
Toll-free (877) BUY BOOK
Local Phone (610) 941-9999
Fax (610) 941-9959
Info@buybooksontheweb.com
www.buybooksontheweb.com

TABLE OF CONTENTS

Acknowledgments i

Chapter
One   Background and Definitions .... 1 - 4

Two   Renewed Interest .... 5 - 13

Three   Three Bible Lessons .... 14 - 22

Four   The Jews, the Holocaust,
             and Black Slavery in the U.S. .... 23 - 31

Five   The Amount and How Spent .... 32 - 42

Six   Who Pays and Who Receives? .... 43 - 52

Seven   The Role of Humanism in the
             Demand for Black Reparation .... 53 - 64

Eight   Heritability .... 65 - 73

Conclusions .... 74 - 76
Appendix A: The Black Manifesto .... 77 - 90
Appendix B: Ten Reasons - David Horowitz .... 91 - 95

Endnotes .... 96 - 101
Bibliography .... 102 - 106
Index .... 107 - 110

ACKNOWLEDGMENTS

All Scripture quotations, unless noted otherwise, are from The New Scofield Study Bible, New King James Version, published in 1989 by Thomas Nelson Publishers, and used by permission.

I am grateful to the Philadelphia Tribune, the Philadelphia Inquirer, the Free Library of Philadelphia (Central, Wadsworth, Northwest Regional, West Oak Lane, Rodriguez, and West Philadelphia Regional branches); the libraries of the Eastern Baptist Theological Seminary, and the Lutheran Theological Seminary. I want to thank Deacon Richard Taylor for the illustration on the front cover; N'COBRA for all their help; Mr. David Horowitz for his "Ten Reasons"; the Reverend James Rivera for his assistance; C. Scribner and Sons for the poem, *Invictus*. And to my wife, Thelma, for her patience with me during the hours of research and writing. May the Lord Jesus Christ be praised!

CHAPTER 1 - BACKGROUND AND DEFINITIONS

The history of black slavery in the United States is not pleasant to read, and there are people who cry, "Enough already!" We are told that to describe this sordid period in the history of America is to pull the scab off of the wound, and to slow the process of race reconciliation. However, to better understand ourselves as a nation, we must not neglect, deny, revise, or seek to hide the facts of this period of our history. Reconciliation is not based upon ignorance.

As for the number of African men, women and children involved in the centuries the slave trade flourished, estimates range from 3.5 million to over 50 million (Lincoln & Mamiya, 237). A common conservative estimate is roughly ten million imported to the Americas, with some two million dying either during capture or the trip across the Atlantic Ocean (the Middle Passage). Add to this figure another fourteen million taken across the Sahara Desert, or sent to North Africa and the Middle East (Sowell,188). The fact remains, the total numbers of Africans taken from the continent will never be known (Faber, 1).

What is known is that by the time of the Revolutionary War blacks constituted nearly 700,000 of the total population of nearly 2,500,000 of the American colonies. Just prior to the Civil War there were 3,953,760 slaves (488,070 free persons) making up nearly one third of the South's population.[1]

It is not easy to retain composure after seeing drawings and reading descriptions of ships jammed with their human cargo. Greed and the love of money are compassionless. The acts of cruelty, brutality, rape, torture, and murder inflicted upon the slaves were unconscionable. All racism is heinous; it is an insult to God our Creator, but religion gives slavery a demonic flavor.

This is said in light of the fact that slaveholders depended more upon the biblical argument than upon any other argument (i.e., economic, political) to support their proslavery theories

(Banks, *Slavery*, 2).

The destruction of family life was horrendous. "Virtually no child was traded with its father, nor wife sold with her husband ... this remarkable process of destruction ... left slaves and the slave community the awful task of repairing and restarting lives ... the categories of the trade [age, color, health, skills, gender: females especially in demand, etc.] were almost custom-built to maximize forcible separations" (Tadman, 133,141).

The effects of slavery did not end with the Emancipation Proclamation. The snap of a finger or the signing of a piece of paper would not erase results of two centuries of bondage. There are those who trace to many present-day ills to slavery. Attributed to slavery are such problems as: low self-esteem, shattered self-images; unemployment; housing restrictions, unequal educational facilities and job opportunities; a welfare mentality; racist religious institutions (boards, schools, churches, Bible institutes, seminaries, conventions); poor health care services; prejudiced media, a criminal justice system that is *not* color blind, and legal maneuvering calculated to maintain an undemocratic and evil status quo.

"Two centuries of slavery and another of discrimination and segregation did indeed produce victims in a world-historical scale. Today's black poverty is the most visible remainder [and reminder] of a history filled with equal measures of pain and shame on the subject of race" (Magnet, 131).

THE AIM OF THE REPARATION MOVEMENT

This leads us to the purpose of the reparation movement. Conrad W. Worrill, chairman of the National Black United Front, defines reparation as "the damages, compensation, and redress of wrongs, so that the countries and people that suffered will enjoy full freedom to continue their own development on more equal terms" (*The Philadelphia Tribune*, 7 March 2001).

The reported goal of reparation is for white Americans to pay slave descendants money for the *un*paid labor in the cotton fields, railroads, etc. Remuneration is also demanded for *under*payment since emancipation. Compensation is to be paid for denying blacks the opportunity to acquire land and natural resources that had been offered and accepted by whites.

In other words, one goal of the reparationist is to provide blacks with that share of the American Pie they would have had, had it not been for slavery. As we shall see, how big that slice should be has not been determined or clearly defined. Although punishment for whites is considered a side result, reparation is believed to relieve or alleviate frustration and the deep sense of victimization experienced by blacks (Barkan, 292).

REPARATION OR REPARATIONS?

Throughout this work I seek to make clear and to maintain the difference between reparation (singular) and reparations (plural). The latter, reparations (plural), is defined as compensation or remuneration required from a defeated *nation* as indemnity for damage or injury during a *war*. "Reparations implies nationhood, which implies territory, which has raised the problem of ghetto colonies scattered around America, without unity or a representative national organization" (Schuchter, 81).

Redress is considered by some scholars a more satisfactory term than *reparations* because it does not have the legal denotation or the link with the concept of territoriality. McGriff (*The Philadelphia Tribune*, 24 April 2001) calls this wrongful quibbling and nitpicking, but as is later pointed out, we do not believe that it is logical to use what Japanese Americans received, or what Israel received from Germany, or Kuwait from Iraq as a basis for demanding money from white Americans, or from the Government of the United States.

The slaves did not constitute a nation, but were taken from different African countries; and America did not lose the war, for it was not at war. And so reparations (plural) is not the correct word to use. We maintain the singular *reparation* is the appropriate word for the compensation sought for the centuries of involuntary servitude of black Africans and their descendants in the United States. Reparation implies giving compensation to satisfy those who suffered injury, loss, or wrong at the hands of another.

Summary: Although the number of Africans taken from the continent is not known, the cruelty of the practice is well documented. All Americans, especially whites, should have some knowledge of this aspect of American history. Without blaming slavery for all of the present-day ills of our society, it is recognized that some contemporary societal problems do have their roots in slavery. The demand of the reparationists is made loud and clear, their goals are broadcast, and increasingly heard, whether or not the distinction between reparation (singular) and reparations (plural) is maintained. It is to this demand that we address our attention.

CHAPTER 2 - RENEWED INTEREST

The matter of reparation for black slave descendants of America has received national attention through network talk shows, news programs, newspapers and magazines. Reparation was featured on *Good Morning America, Today, Crossfire, Phil Donahue, Morton Downey, Jr.,* and in *The Boston Globe, Washington Post, USA Today, Newsweek* (Barkan, 382n3). City councils in Detroit, Chicago, Dallas, Cleveland, Washington, D.C., passed bills supporting establishing a commission to study the black reparation issue.

Illustrative of the renewed interest in black reparation are the many overwhelmingly negative comments derived from a variety of sources: "I object to being declared guilty by association" -- "Asking people to atone for sins that someone else committed makes a mockery of justice."

"I just don't like black people!" -- "Black Reparation is reverse discrimination" -- "It is an attempt to produce a sense of guilt on white Americans" -- "Duck and chuck the whole issue, and move on!" -- "Reparation has been paid already with affirmative action programs, welfare, black history month (February), plea bargaining, section 8 vouchers, and federal school lunch programs! What more do you want?"

"It is a dumb idea, a stupid proposal" -- "preposterous junk, trash, rubbish" -- "there are irreconcilable differences between the races, between black and white Americans" -- "Demagoguery about racial reparations will embitter reasonable people, and increase the resistance of those on the fringes" -- "Common sense tells us there is nobody in the world who could not sue somebody, somewhere, sometime, somehow, for something done wrong."

"Government intervention is socialism, a form of government that only worsens conditions" -- "Black Americans today would still be in Africa, one tribe fighting another, like they're doing over

there now, if there had been no slavery." -- "Reparation is nothing but a growing movement of politically correct victimhood" -- "The more we emphasize our racial, religious and political differences, the more we divide ourselves into special groups."
"Letting Uncle Sam redistribute money from one group to another group is a liberal cure-all attempt to solve societal problems" -- "Waste of time dwelling on conditions we are incapable of changing" -- "Reparation is a highfalutin' term for government-controlled super affirmative action" -- "will do irreparable harm to race relationships in America."
"Reparation has a huge potential for increasing racial strife " -- "Reconciliation is a one-on-one matter. Wholesale political or financial remedies cannot help but fail" -- "Paternalism is the father of reparation; blacks are treated like children" -- " When justice is measured in terms of money, the concept of justice is diminished" -- "It is impossible to assess or remedy injuries resulting from segregation" -- "What about all the other evils in this imperfect world for which there is no compensation or redress?"

The following comments also have helped to keep the issue roiling. Linda Chavez, president of the conservative Center for Equal Opportunity, in Washington, D.C., said the attempt to pay what is called "the debt of the past" is a "recipe for hatred," and can only cause "as many difficulties as it alleviates."
Glen Loury called the reparation movement "bad politics." He added that contractual remuneration will not change American blacks' second-class citizenship status, eliminate ghettos, eradicate racial profiling, or decrease black incarceration. "The challenge," he said, "is much more fundamental than demanding reparations" (*The Philadelphia Inquirer,* 27 Mar 2001).

THE BLACK MANIFESTO

What's behind this renewed interest? The idea of reparation is not new. Over thirty years ago, *The Black Manifesto* stirred up the waters (See Appendix A). At that time, Dr. J.H. Jackson called the Black Manifesto a "totalitarian message" which would "destroy religious freedom." Rustin said, "Guilt is an uncomfortable emotion, and the guilty party will rationalize his sins and affirm them as virtues. By such a process today's ally can become tomorrow's enemy" (*Ebony*, 101). "It's another form of hustle," said Rustin (*Newsweek*, 31).

James Forman led a protest at the liberal Riverside Church in New York City, at which time this former chairman of SNCC (Student Nonviolent Coordinating Committee) presented to the church a Black Manifesto that demanded $500 million, among other things, from white churches and synagogues. This original amount later was raised by Forman on 13 June 1969, to $3 billion.

The writers of this manifesto charged Christian churches with a "collective guilt" for their "complicity in black enslavement and destruction or even for the essentially segregated character of Christianity in modern times" (Schuchter, xi). The demand made for reparation by the manifesto is interpreted as one more attempt to assert "revolutionary black nationalism and the nationhood of blacks" (Schuchter, 81).

The Manifesto's writers and supporters are especially taken to task for their attack upon religious institutions. Whereas many blame Christianity for numerous evils in regard to the slaves, and insist the missionaries were sent in first to soften up the Africans so the military could take over, the fact remains that some whites recognized their obligations as Christians, and took advantage of the opportunity to witness for Christ. Had it not been for the genuine white Christian, the plight of the blacks would have been much worse (Banks, *Black Church,* 115).

And the role of the "Black Church" must not be forgotten. It has given race leadership, strengthened family life, and, as a social center, has provided fellowship, shelter, and mutual aid. Without such an outlet under the circumstances that prevailed in slavery, much more blood would have been shed and the spiritual progress of America as a whole hindered all the more. Schuchter (58) adds: "Short of armed rebellion, the Black Manifesto contains no program that offers any hope of blunting the devastating impact of racism and the power of white paternalism."

MUHAMMAD KENYATTA

One of the signers of the Black Manifesto was the Reverend Muhammad Kenyatta, born Donald Brooks Jackson in Chester, Pa. A religious prodigy, he was called to preach at the age of 12, and at 14 he delivered his first sermon. Called the "The Boy Wonder Preacher" during his high school days, he preached nearly every Sunday at his uncle's church, the Solid Rock Baptist Church in South Philadelphia. Kenyatta was a militant civil rights preacher who confronted white churches in the Philadelphia area with reparation demands.

On 18 May 1969, two weeks after the Black Manifesto had been presented by the Black Economic Development Conference, the 25-year old Kenyatta walked into St. Anthony's Roman Catholic Church in Chester, and presented demands for reparation.

When he confronted a white suburban church and dumped the elements used to celebrate the Lord's Supper (Communion), *The Philadelphia Inquirer* published this Letter, 13 Jan 1970:

'Death Warrant'
Sir:
   Christians are warned not to eat and drink of the Communion table in an unworthy manner, lest they trifle with the death of Christ and suffer the penalty of weakness, sickness and even death (1 Cor. 11.29, 30).
   Surely Muhammad Kenyatta has signed his own death warrant by throwing communion bread and wine on the floor of the Swarthmore Presbyterian Church. How shocking!

I am sure that all Bible believers who are black will agree that Kenyatta does not speak for us. We view his action as nothing less than desecration. In demonstrating what he termed "the extent of black anger," he has incurred upon himself the wrath of God, an anger before which no man shall stand -- even if he is black!

Sincerely Yours,
Wm. L. Banks
Pastor, Nazarene Baptist Church

Muhammad Kenyatta died of heart failure in January, 1992, at the age of 47, while waiting for a kidney transplant. "There is a way that seems right to a man, but its end is the way of death" (Proverbs 14.12). [1]

THE MOVEMENT GROWS

Today we find the movement gathering momentum after decades of feeble attempts to be taken more seriously. Some men have argued for the moral justification of reparation, but felt the movement lacks political feasibility. Lecky and Wright (94) state that the time for reparation is now, although "it is dangerous to predict what might become feasible in the near future."

It has been "on the public agenda, or just below it, since the mid-nineties" (Barkan, 283). In fact, John Conyers, Jr., Detroit Representative, called an "unabashed liberal," has quietly championed black reparation for years. Since 1989 he repeatedly filed legislation calling for a national commission to consider the possibility of reparation to the descendants of black slaves.[2] Increasing numbers of politicians, preachers, intellectuals and civil rights groups believe the reparation movement is an opportunity for the government to address and implement its role in continuing combating racial inequities in our society.

There are a number of reasons why reparation receives the attention now it has not gotten in the past. Indeed, a combination of symbolic, psychological, social and material components motivate the renewed demand, as a new generation of legal and political activists has rallied to the cause. For one thing, the movement has been stimulated in part by the success of other groups who have been compensated for past injustices. American blacks watched with growing resentment as other groups received apologies or restitution from various governments.

EXAMPLES OF RESTITUTION

1. Between the years 1942 and 1946, approximately 120,000 Japanese (two-thirds of them Japanese-American citizens) were interned by the United States government. It was felt that they were national security risks during World War II. African Americans felt shortchanged, cheated, deprived by the fact the Nisei (second generation Japanese) received $20,000 apiece (total amounting to $1.25 billion) in 1988. In 1992 it was agreed upon by the U.S. Office of Reparations to increase the amounts to the Nisei or their descendants (cf. Munford, 414).

2. The victims of Nazi slave labor, and Jewish Holocaust survivors collected nearly $60 billion from Germany. In addition they sought the return of looted wealth stashed away in Switzerland by the Nazis; they also sought the return of wealth legitimately deposited in Swiss banks by Jews. Germany used "Switzerland as its major source of foreign currency during the war, but also shipped many of its treasures there, most often in the form of gold bars and artworks, to be held in safekeeping for after the war" (Barkan, 89).[3]

3. American Indians received an apology from the Bureau of Indian Affairs. As much as $1 trillion, including land and benefits, may have been paid to Native Americans.[4]

4. Korean "comfort women" sought reparation from Japan ($1 billion in 1994). They had been sex slaves of the Japanese soldiers during World War II. The name *comfort women* is "the official name given by the Japanese army to the military's organization and forced prostitution in organized brothels" (Barkan, 47), operated by the Japanese, especially in Korea, as well as in China and the Philippines.

5. Other cases include the Aborigines from Australia; Kuwait vs. Iraq; the Inuits from Canada. And about $10 million in reparation was given out to descendants of the Tuskegee syphilis ("bad blood") experiments. In 1997 a Race Riot Commission was set up to investigate and consider reparation for the survivors of the May 31-June 1, 1921 race riot in Tulsa, Oklahoma. As many as 300 people may have been murdered (figures vary). In the year 2000 the Tulsa Commission recommended that reparation be paid.

6. In 1994, Governor Lawton Chiles of Florida signed a law giving $2.1 million to the descendants of the 1923 rampage by a white mob on the mostly black hamlet of Rosewood of two hundred blacks. The town was wiped out, destroyed. After losing livelihoods and homes, the blacks never returned. What they left behind was "acquired" by local whites.[5]

These examples of recent governmental apologies and remuneration are cited in answer to those anti-reparationists who argue that black slave exploitation occurred too long ago for restitution to be made now (Robinson, 224, 225). In addition we are told that slavery did not end in 1865, but "having sown to the wind, America now reaps the whirlwind," and the terrible conditions of the post-Reconstruction era have extended themselves, however modified, into the present age.

ROBINSON'S BOOK, *THE DEBT*

Randall Robinson is the former president of TransAfrica, an organ-ization that played a major role in America's battle against apartheid in South Africa. His book, *The Debt, What America Owes to Blacks,* has also pushed the reparation issue into the limelight. Many American citizens have come to realize the deep social and psychological impact slavery has made upon this country. They understand that no amount of money or restitution of property could compensate for the suffering, pain, heartbreak, family disruption, torture, and all such intangibles.

There is no accurate assessment of the economic value of such losses. It is contrary to the teachings of the Bible to believe that apologies and financial compensation provide mechanisms for healing the present social and economic troubles. So the matter of black reparation has also sparked renewed interest in the reading of the Bible in the search for what we believe is the will of God.

HOROWITZ'S *TEN REASONS*

Without doubt one reason for the renewed interest in black reparation is the work of David Horowitz, entitled: **Ten Reasons Why Reparations for Blacks Is a Bad Idea** *for Blacks* **and Racist Too.** See Appendix B. Basically, I concur with Horowitz that black reparation is indeed "a bad idea." Having said this, note several ideas broached by Horowitz with which I disagree.[6]

In Reason #3, the statement that 350,000 Union soldiers died to set free the black slaves is suspect. It is doubtful that this was the motive, primary or otherwise, of the majority of Union soldiers. Freeing slaves was not the major goal of the North. Preserving the Union, preventing secession, maintaining political and economic power were issues more important. Fighting and winning the war resulted in the freedom of the slaves, but emancipation was not the cause for which they gave their lives (Johnson, 460).[7]

In Reason # 9, Horowitz makes claims for whites which are quite broad. For one thing, Abraham Lincoln did not give "his life to sign the Emancipation Proclamation."[8] He was assassinated, just as Martin Luther King, Jr. was slain. Neither one voluntarily gave his life for a noble cause. Horowitz is guilty of the same kind of inflated rhetoric of which blacks stand accused. God used white Englishmen and Americans to bring a halt to the slave trade, but this is not the same as saying it "would not have been brought to an end" had it not been for them. That's a bit too much to say. It's in the same category with a statement like, "Had it not been for M.L. King, Jr., (or Rosa Parks) we would still be riding in the back of the bus."

Summary: More than thirty years ago interest in black reparation was sparked by the introduction of the Black Manifesto. In more recent days talk shows, newspapers (articles, letters), and magazines, have featured proposals, advocates, critics on this issue. Payments to the Nisei, Israel, Holocaust victims, and others have caused the voices of black reparationists to be heard. Congressman John Conyers' repeated efforts, Randall Robinson's book, *The Debt*, and David Horowitz's *Ten Reasons* have all caused the lime-light to fall upon the issue of black reparation.

CHAPTER 3 - THREE BIBLICAL LESSONS

THE EXODUS

Exodus 12.35,36: *Now the children of Israel had done according to the word of Moses, and they had asked from the Egyptians articles of silver, articles of gold, and clothing. And the LORD had given the people favor in the sight of the Egyptians, so that they granted them what they requested. Thus they plundered the Egyptians.*

Psalm 105.37,38: *He also brought them out with silver and gold, and there was none feeble among His tribes. Egypt was glad when they departed, for the fear of them had fallen upon them.*

These passages celebrate the miraculous deliverance and departure of the Israelites from the land of Egypt. Marching out as a victorious army, they enriched themselves with a substantial amount of gold, silver, and raiment. Centuries earlier, God had said to Abram that his descendants would be strangers in a foreign land, serve them, and be afflicted four hundred years. But the Lord will judge that nation, and the descendants of Abram "will come out with great possessions" (Genesis 15.13,14).

This theme of restoration is repeated twice more:
(1) In Exodus 3.21, 22, the Lord told Moses He would give the Israelites favor in the eyes of the Egyptians, and the Jews would not leave the land empty-handed. Indeed, Egypt would be despoiled of gold, silver, and clothing.

(2) Then in Exodus 11.1, 2, the Lord gave Moses further reassurance of divine judgment against Egypt, and guaranteed a prosperous exodus for the Israelites.
After the ten plagues -- blood, frogs, gnats, flies, livestock

pestilence, boils, hail, locusts, darkness, death of the firstborn -- the Egyptians urged the Israelites to make haste and leave the country. The Hebrew word translated *were urged* (Exodus 12.33) may be rendered, "strongly encouraged," "pressed." It is derived from a verb meaning to be or grow firm, strong, strengthen (*Brown, Driver, Briggs,* 304). Fear moved the Egyptians to plead, "Leave! For otherwise we shall all be dead. Having killed our firstborn, will we be next? Yea, we too are exposed to death!"

Having obeyed Moses, the children of Israel had asked for (not *borrowed*) the spoil, and what they requested, the Egyptians freely gave or granted (not *lent*). Use of the words spoil or plunder sounds too strong to the modern ear. Usually the word *spoil* makes us think of booty legally taken from a conquered people. Internationally, it is lawful to spoil and plunder an enemy. Force or rapine is implied by the word *spoil.* Albeit moved by fear, the Egyptians gave freely of their gold, silver, and clothing.

What the Jews received is looked upon as just recompense for the centuries of toil in Egypt, the years of labor for which they received very low wages or none at all. The material possessions given may be seen as the recovery of wages unjustly held back by the Egyptians.

Keep in mind, however, that what occurred was at God's direction. So the spoiling of Egypt was not a criminal act. The God of the Bible is Sovereign. He has the right to do as He pleases, and because He is God, He can do nothing unholy. So that no injustice was done to the Pharaoh or his people. As the avowed enemies of God's people, the idolatrous Egyptians had exploited the Jews for some four hundred years. And now Israel is rewarded for its long compulsory labor.

Indeed, considering what Joseph had accomplished (Genesis, chapters 37-50), Egypt owed much of its wealth, influence, and political existence to the Israelites.

EXODUS COMPARED WITH BLACK SLAVERY

How does this event stack up with the demand for reparation by black Americans? There is little similarity:

(1) The nation of Israel was in slavery in Egypt for more than 400 years; black slaves from various nations and tribes toiled in America for approximately 246 years. Do not add the years of segregation and Jim Crow, for what the Jewish people have suffered throughout the years far outweighs the racism experienced by black Americans.

(2) What Moses and Israel did in spoiling Egypt was directed by Jehovah. The black reparation movement has no such Sponsor.

(3) God gave the Israelites favor in the sight of the Egyptians. Most white Americans are not in sympathy with the black reparation movement.

(4) The evidently vast amounts of gold, silver and clothing given to the newly freed Israelite slaves sadly contrasts with the failed offer to newly freed blacks of "forty acres and a mule."

(5) The Exodus (literally, *way out*) has God's people leaving Egypt. Most reparationists plan to remain in America. Plans to return to Liberia, or to some other country in Africa, or to set up a state or another country within the United States, have had very little support. The dreams of Marcus Garvey, Elijah Muhammad, and others were never fulfilled.

(6) The spoiling deals with Israelites who physically left Egypt, *not* with their descendants. Black reparation is intended for descendants of black slaves. The American Colonization Society

(official name: *The American Society for the Colonization of Free People of Color*) was formed in 1816-1817, under the leadership of the Presbyterian minister, Robert S. Finley. Its primary aim of colonization, with Congressional approval, was to remove the free blacks, and those who would become free in a territory, and send them back to Africa.

There were about one and a half million blacks in the U.S. in 1816, of whom approximately thirteen percent were free. Approximately 12,000 slaves were actually colonized and went to the continent, primarily to Liberia. Suffice it to say, the goals of the Colonization Society created little enthusiasm among the blacks.

Southern blacks did not object to colonization in the same manner as did the Northern blacks, but object they did. It is said that a white missionary offered a black slave an opportunity to return to Africa. The slave replied, "I crossed the ocean once, but I made up my mind then never to trust myself in a boat with a white man again." Free blacks were never enthusiastic about the Society. In general, blacks considered colonization a scheme to re-enslave them.[1]

ZACCHAEUS

Luke 19.8: *Then Zacchaeus stood and said to the Lord, "Look, Lord, I give half of my goods to the poor; and if I have taken anything from anyone by false accusation, I restore fourfold."* This story is used by some black reparationists to support their goal. It is stated, for example, that "reparation is part of the gospel message. Zacchaeus knew well the necessity for repayment as an essential ingredient in repentance" (Cone, and Wilmore, 130). Our study reveals that Zacchaeus was an "up and outer" -- up a tree and out on a limb. He was a "come-shorter" (Romans 3.23).

Because he worked as a chief tax collector for the Roman government, he was hated by his fellow Jewish citizens. From their point of view he was a traitor. Furthermore, typical of the tax collectors of that day, Zacchaeus took for himself a percentage of what was demanded by the government. Though the name Zacchaeus means *pure*, his dealings were anything but pure.

As the story unfolds, the Lord Jesus spotted this "Commissioner of Taxes," who had climbed up into a sycamore tree to see the Lord. "Zacchaeus, make haste and come down, for today I must stay at your house." He immediately obeyed. It is believed the conversation and personal fellowship with Christ led to the conversion of Zacchaeus.

Because of his change of heart he publicly announced after dinner his intention to make restitution -- indeed, one of the strongest verses in the New Testament on the subject. The taker was now a giver.

Restoration does not eliminate guilt, but what Zacchaeus proposed is evidence his heart was made right with God. Christ could now say of him, "Today salvation has come to this house, because he (Zacchaeus) also is a son of Abraham" (Luke 19.9). We are not told Zacchaeus quit his job as a tax collector, but we assume he no longer cheated people.

The words, "and if I have taken anything" (Luke 19.8) have caused some problems of interpretation. But scholars (Alford, Tenney, Lenski, MacDonald, Plummer, et al) assure us there is no uncertainty in the expression. *If* here means whatever, or better, since. The conditional Greek sentence implies Zacchaeus knew he was guilty of extortion. "If, as I know is the case" (Plummer, *ICC*), signifies that no hypothesis is intended. It is a condition of reality. He assumed he had cheated or "pressed money out" of someone by false assertions.

While Zacchaeus was in accord with Hebrew standards of rectitude, he imposed upon himself a severer penalty, one which was more in line with destructive robbery. According to Exodus 22.1, if a man steals an ox or a sheep, and kills it or sells it, he shall restore five oxen for an ox, and four sheep for a sheep (cf. 2 Samuel 12.6, where David replies to the prophet Nathan). So ordinarily, the law for restoration required the full value plus 20 percent (Leviticus 6.5; Numbers 5.7). Some cases required simple restoration (1 Samuel 12.3); or double restitution (Exodus 22.4,7). And Proverbs 6.31 speaks of sevenfold exaction. Other verses dealing with restoration or redress are 2 Kings 8.6; Ezekiel 33.15.

Now can we appeal to this incident to support black reparation? I think not. There is a biblical basis for reparation, as we have seen, but it does not help the black reparationist. The Bible surely teaches we reap what we sow. Judgment is guaranteed by the resurrection of Jesus Christ (Acts 17.31).

Zacchaeus was a Jew, under the Law, well aware of the teachings concerning restitution. He repaid those he directly cheated, **not** their descendants. Motivated by his spiritual relationship with Jesus Christ, what he did was done voluntarily out of personal conviction. In fact, he *overdid* it! We dare not put one man, Zacchaeus, on a level with the more than 260 million Americans. The demand for reparation is highly impersonal and amounts to guilt by association. It leaps over generations and indicts the entire white population.

Zacchaeus repaid those whom he had swindled; blacks seek reparation from whites. He voluntarily did so; most white Americans resist the movement, and desire not to give one red cent! Zacchaeus was a believer; most folks in the United States are not genuine Christians, professing or possessing. Indeed, there is no such animal as a "Christian nation." Finally, note that Zacchaeus was deeply concerned about the poor.

JAMES 5.4

Indeed the wages of the laborers who mowed your fields, which you kept back by fraud, cry out; and the cries of the reapers have reached the ears of the Lord of Sabaoth.

James teaches that God will judge rich oppressors. Rotted riches, moth-eaten garments, corroded gold and silver are the miseries awaiting them. The rich must not think that the Lord is an uninterested Spectator of the affairs of men. One reason why the wealthy treasure up judgment fire for themselves is their injustice to their farm laborers. The *fields* upon which they worked are not small plots of ground, but "the whole estate under one ownership," a large tract of cultivated ground (Ropes, 288).

The text speaks of the workers who reaped, cut or mowed down and gathered, but the plowing and sowing by the same workers might be considered. And for all their work their rich employers kept back their wages by fraud. They defrauded or robbed the workers, or withheld their wages; "both could apply perfectly here" (Zodhiates, part 3, 66).

How readily comes to mind the lot of sharecroppers in America! Very early in man's history this frequently occurring sin was noted in the Old Testament and condemned. It is bad enough that these men are busy cheating in their business deals, overreaching in greed, scheming and lying, and tricking other businessmen, but to deal so shabbily with lowly workers is another matter.

You shall not defraud (cheat) your neighbor, nor rob him. The wages of him who is hired shall not remain with you all night until morning ... You shall not oppress a hired servant who is poor and needy ... Each day you shall give him his wages, and not let the sun go down on it.[2]

Here we see that God condemns using service without paying

wages; and repeatedly states that the laborer is worthy of his hire.[3] Note the Hebraistic concept of having inanimate things "cry out." In Genesis 4.10, the blood of slain Abel cries out to God from the ground. The depravity of Sodom and Gomorrah cries out to God (Genesis 18.20, 19.13). The stone cries out from the wall (Habakkuk 2.11).

And now the wages fraudulently held back (permanently) shout (continually) as if with a loud voice, and the repeated cries reach the ears of the Lord of Sabaoth. This title of God, used in the New Testament only here and Romans 9.29, means Lord of Hosts. The hosts include not only the armies of Israel, but also angels, the sun, moon and stars of heaven; locusts and worms; wind and rain; rivers and oceans (and fish).

He commands them all to do His bidding. In short, "the meaning of the title is that all created agencies and forces are under the leadership or dominion of Jehovah, who made and maintains them." So the title Lord of Hosts signifies God's almighty power by which He governs. As Lord of Hosts He punishes the wicked.

Men must not imagine the poor have no defender. James 5.4 gives us one more argument against slavery, especially that brand that was practiced in the United States. The Bible condemns all acquisition of riches by dishonest means (Jeremiah 17.11). "If the rebuke in this one passage of the Word of God were regarded, slavery would at once come to an end" (Barnes, 355).

However, keep in mind that James deals with hired hands, not slaves. Fraud is fraud, but intentionally failing to keep a promise to pay the wages depends on the relationship between employer and employees. In a negotiated contract, the parties are expected to fulfill their obligation. However, the slavery practiced in the United States was not based upon employer-employee relationships. No contracts were made with slaves.[4] A slave is a slave is a slave.

With such control over the life of a man, there is no such thing as *unpaid* labor. The slavemaster feeds and clothes the slave only because it is profitable to do so; it is good for his *investment*. The point is not to make slavery an innocent, humane institution, but to caution using this passage in the book of James as a basis for demanding black reparation.

Summary: We find examples of reparation in the Bible, but no basis for giving remuneration to the descendants of black slavery in America. In all three Bible passages: (1) the Jews leaving Egypt (2) Zacchaeus and those whom he had defrauded (3) those laborers whose wages had been withheld -- remuneration was for contemporaries, not descendants. The Egyptians were "prodded" to give voluntarily; Zacchaeus gave willingly; the rich in James were warned of the dire consequences for failure to obey the Lord of Sabaoth.

In each case God personally intercedes on behalf of the downtrodden, the cheated. Jehovah moved upon both Egyptians and Israelites to fulfill his promise; the Lord Jesus personally entered the life of Zacchaeus; and James used God's Word to directly warn the double-minded, unbelieving Jews of judgment (Lenski, 644).

CHAPTER 4 - THE JEWS, THE HOLOCAUST AND BLACK SLAVERY IN THE UNITED STATES

THE PART PLAYED BY JEWS

In recent years Mr. Louis Farrakhan, head of the Nation of Islam or Black Muslims, accused the Jewish people of playing a big part in the American slave trade. S.E. Anderson (21) also charges the Jews with being very deeply involved in the *business* of slave trading. He cites David Brion Davis, who states in his book, *The Slave Trade and the Jews*, that directly or indirectly, many Jewish businesses and merchants participated in the slave trade.

It is not denied that Jews participated in the slave trade. Although precise statistics are difficult to find, the fact is that Jews did **not** play a large part in black slavery in the U.S. Despite Farrakhan's accusations that Jews dominated the black slave trade, it would be difficult "to find more than one or two Jewish slave traders in the Anglo-Saxon traffic" (Thomas, 12).

Thomas also points out that it "is true that much of the slave trade in the sixteenth and seventeenth centuries in Lisbon was financed by converted Jews, New Christians, or *conversos*; though whether such a person is to be seen as a Jew is not something on which I should wish to pronounce."

And so it is well known that Jews invested in companies engaged in the slave trade, owned slave ships, and owned slaves (Faber, 2). Within the United States itself, Jews who lived in the South accepted the practice as part of everyday life. There were indeed a small number of Jewish planters in the old South.[1] However, there were few Jews in the rural areas; they felt safer in urban areas.

Jews were more active as peddlers and storekeepers. Those Jews who owned slaves used them as maids, butlers, housekeepers, or as laborers in their various trades. Their slaves were also hired out (Rosen, 15). Jews found the South more hospitable than the North. Southern Jews who had slaves pointed out that Abraham, Isaac, Jacob, and Job also had slaves.²

They were also taught that "the law of the land is the law," and since they lived in a slaveholding society, it was appropriate to accept the status quo. "Northern Jews perceived Southern Jews as proslavery and pro-secession ... Opponents of slavery, Jewish or Gentile, were a distinct minority even in the North. While there were many Jews in the North who actively opposed slavery, few Jews were conspicuous as abolitionists" (Rosen, 35,37, 390n95).

JEWS PLAYED NO LARGE PART IN THE SLAVE TRADE

Faber's study reveals that the Jews did not own slaves in excess of their proportion among white Gentiles; and their participation in the slave trade had little impact. Claims by the Nation of Islam (Farrakhan) that Jews financed the slave trade, and also owned fully 75 percent of all slaves in the South prior to the Civil War are *false* (Faber, 7). As a matter of fact, free blacks owned by far more slaves than Southern Jews did (Rosen, 16).³

The American Jewish community generally avoided the debate over slavery in the antebellum years. As Rosen (389n95) points out, the Jewish community, anxious to assimilate and be accepted, suspicious of the abolitionist movement, was too small, too vulnerable, too insecure in their social, political, and economic strength, and too foreign to affect the outcome of the slave trade. It is true that in the British slave trade, Jews were "investors, importers, exporters, factors, and owners, but in no segment of the business of slavery did they stand out, save for the exceptions of

Alexandre Lindo in Jamaica and Jacob Rodrigues Rivera and Aaron Lopez in Rhode Island. However, even in these instances the overall impact of the Jewish population in the colonies was marginal" (Faber, 143). In summary: Jews participated in the slave trade and ownership, but not in the numbers or degree which their accusers contend.

THE HOLOCAUST

The word *holocaust* literally means "whole burning." It is the designation for the genocide of European Jewry ordered and implemented by the Nazi regime (Herf, 398). "Totality of destruction has been central to the meaning of *holocaust* since it first appeared in Middle English in the 14th century and referred to the biblical sacrifice in which a male animal was wholly burnt on the altar in worship of God" (*American Heritage Dictionary*).

The Greek term means "that which is completely burnt ...Holocaust has also been used to translate ... another Hebrew word used to summarize the genocide of Jews by the Nazis. This sense of *holocaust* has since broadened to include the mass slaughter of other peoples, but when capitalized it refers specifically to the destruction of Jews and other Europeans by the Nazis and may also encompass the Nazi persecution of Jews that preceded the outbreak of the war" (*AHD*).

All racism is demonic, but anti-Semitism is especially devilish. Satan hates all people, but especially detests the Jews. He has good reason, of course. The main reason is that Jesus Christ was a Jew, after the flesh; and the human authors of the Bible were Jewish, and Satan hates the Word of God. Only Luke the physician, who wrote the Gospel of Luke and the book of Acts, was a Gentile.

We know from the Bible that the Jews lived in slavery in Egypt for more than 400 years. Moses led them out of Egypt, and the Old Testament presents a constant reminder by God of His deliverance. The Israelites were again scattered by king Nebuchadnezzar of Babylon, and his armies. Jerusalem's temple was destroyed in 586 B.C. Many people died, and great numbers of Jews were taken captive to Babylonia.

Though many Jews returned from the exile to Judah, still others scattered to live throughout the world. This scattering is called the *diaspora*. Next came the persecution and slaughter of Jews under Antiochus Epiphanes IV of Syria (168-167 B.C.). Jews living in Judea under Roman domination faced severe persecution, and in 70 A.D. Jerusalem was conquered, the temple destroyed again, and many Jews were taken captive to Rome.

"The number of Jewish people killed then was roughly equal in proportion to the number killed in the Holocaust ... proportionately speaking, the percentage of Jewish people who died in that destruction was relatively the same as the percentage who perished at the hands of Hitler" (Kalisher, 29).

During the Middle Ages religious persecution of the Jews increased. The military expedition called the *Crusades* caused a renewal of anti-Semitism. Because the Jews were a minority in every country, they were blamed for whatever economic trouble that country had, and were persecuted.

The areas they were forced to live in were called ghettos. Almost all of the Jews living in England and France were forced out of these countries during the 1200s and 1300s. Spain expelled them in 1492. The Inquisition was established by Spain and Jews and others were tortured and slain. In the late 1900s once again anti-Semitism became a powerful political force in Europe.

Thousands of Jews in Poland, Russia, Germany, Austria-Hungary were killed in a series of massacres called *pogroms*. In 1933 Adolf Hitler came to power in Germany. Jews were forced out of teaching positions, property seized, synagogues destroyed, and thousands of them were sent to concentration camps. When World War II began in 1939, the Nazis conquered nation after nation, and Hitler sought to eliminate the Jews in each country. It is estimated six to ten million Jews were killed, about one million of them were children.

One other comment on this issue. Our interpretation of the Bible leads us to conclude that what has happened to Israel in the past is but a foretaste of its future affliction. Jeremiah 30.7: *"Alas! For that day is great, so that none is like it; and it is the time of Jacob's trouble, but he shall be saved out of it."* This period of tribulation will fall upon the earth after the true Church is translated. The last half of this period includes the unleashing of unprecedented demonic activity.

"The Children of Israel had suffered with various degrees of intensity since their captivity in Babylon. The Scriptures reveal that the future will bring forth a time of trouble for Jacob -- the Jewish people -- that will be more severe than anything that nation has known, more, even, than the nation suffers in these days" (Pilgrim Bible, Jeremiah 30.7). Today there is no peace in the Middle East. Daily Jews and Palestinians are killed, and the strife threatens all out war.

I was an occupation soldier in Germany after the Second World War, and saw with my own eyes the devastation of that land. Germany brought destruction upon itself, having sown to the wind of anti-Semitism, it reaped the whirlwind of devastation. The nation has paid nearly $60 billion to Holocaust survivors.[4] Israel was given $820 million by Germany for the resettlement of 500,000 people.

Presently there are Jews who seek from Switzerland the return of wealth looted from the Jews and deposited there for safe keeping (Barnett, 1072). Suit also has been brought against those corporations that directly profited from the use of Nazi forced labor camps. Claims for reparation by American blacks has been stimulated anew because of these payments by Germany to Israel and to Jewish survivors of the *Holocaust,* or their descendants.[5]

Herf (91,92) brings to our attention the objections raised by the Eastern zone of Germany to restitution (*wiedergutmachung: making good again*) to Jewish survivors of the Holocaust. A more sympathetic ear was found in West Germany (Herf, 3,50,51). If Americans balk at giving reparation to the descendants of a slave society that ended 136 years ago, imagine Germans unwilling to make restitution to present-day Jewish *survivors* of the Holocaust.

In a poll of 1,000 Germans, 45 percent said they were tired of hearing about the atrocities of Nazi Germany; and some 46 percent felt that Nazism was not all bad, but had some good sides as well. Many Germans complained they were sick of repeatedly hearing about the Holocaust. They felt no guilt or responsibility, and had no desire to be held prisoner of their past, although the public survey revealed wide support for compensating slave laborers of the Nazi era.

To top matters off, some 80 percent felt that "only a small minority of Germans were anti-Semitic." Some 61 percent agreed that one should not pull the scab off old wounds suffered in the Hitler era.[6] And so, Germans, not sixty years away from the horrors of world War II, have no desire to atone for the Holocaust. What makes black Americans think that white Americans have any desire to express remorse and remunerate the descendants of an enslavement that took place more than 136 years ago?

Listen again to some of the remarks made by the Germans: "Why give anything to the Jews leaving Germany? These emigres no longer have any claim on Germany"... "Jewish capitalists are strengthened when we recognize their right to have damage replaced"... "German refugees receive nothing, so why should the Jews?" "The Jews must also share in the general impoverishment brought about by the war" (Herf, 91). Lawsuits brought against German companies by the United States caused a fight over a $4.6 billion fund. For many years German companies had denied any responsibility for using slave labor. They claimed they used such laborers because the Nazis forced them to do so. Geir Mouson (*The Philadelphia Inquirer,* 31 May 2001, A9) points out German lawmakers finally agreed to payments to workers forced into labor during World War II by the Nazis. It is expected that more than a million forced and slave workers will receive payments.

REACTIONS

Consider now some of the reactions of the reparationists and of the anti-reparationists. Several things stick in the craw of blacks demanding redress. One is the interesting fact that "Jewish agencies were specially inhospitable to reparation to black economic development, a factor noted as ironic by observers of several persuasions since Jews in modern history have received 'financial amends.' It was not considered an answer to the inequalities and injustices of our society."[7]

Another matter is the establishment of the Holocaust museum in Washington, D.C. Barkan (292) states success of the museum "has instigated resentment among certain African Americans. The resentment is a result, on the one hand, of wishing to emulate it and, on the other, of seeing it as a symbol of the Jews' ability to construct the public view of Jewish history and corner the market on suffering, which implicitly leaves African Americans behind."

Of course, the major bone of contention is the fact that the nation of Israel, as well as individual Jews, have received reparations, while black descendants of slaves in American have received nothing. Those opposed to giving reparation point out there is no comparison between the suffering of the Jews and the suffering of the blacks. Randall Robinson (216) states that the "black holocaust is far and away the most heinous human rights crime visited upon any group of people in the world over the last five hundred years." It is interesting that he adds the caveat, "over the last five hundred years." For reparationists who may desire to omit this qualification, attention is directed to the larger picture of the suffering of the Jewish people.[8]

Now in comparing the Jewish *Holocaust* with black slavery in the U.S., a number of things should be considered:

(1) It is not accurate to compare the less than twenty years under Hitler with the 246 years of black slavery in America. What occurred in Nazi Germany was but the latest exhibition of the demonic nature of anti-Semitism. As we have shown, the suffering of the Jewish people did not begin with the *Holocaust*.

(2) The Jews were citizens of Germany, and of the other European countries in which they lived; the black slaves in America were not citizens.

(3) It was the purpose of the Nazis to exterminate the Jews; but the slave traders for the most part sought to preserve the lives of the slaves. To the plantation owners, slaves were money. Money was their motive. Slaves were economically valuable to the plantation owners.[9]

(4) Jews were robbed of their material possessions; the slaves had none. Both however were deprived of their dignity, selfhood, families and freedom.

(5) More than a half century has passed, there are still Holocaust survivors, "identifiable individuals whose experience of the ultimate injustice was direct" (Reed, 17). All of the blacks who lived as slaves in America are dead.

Summary: Records show that Jews indeed played a part in the American slave trade, but their role was not nearly as great as some blacks would make it. Technically, the word *Holocaust* refers to the attempt of Nazi Germany to "wholly burn" or exterminate the Jewish people. A study of history shows that anti-Semitism is nothing new, and the total picture of Jewish suffering is greater than that of any other one group of people.

Recently, voices from Germany have demonstrated their opposition to reparations to Jewish survivors or to Israel. And have expressed their desire that the matter be put to rest. Finally, it is pointed out to black reparationists that their resentment towards Jewish reparations has no logical basis, and the comparison of black slavery with the *Holocaust* should not be sought as a reason for demanding black reparation.

CHAPTER 5 - THE AMOUNT AND HOW SPENT

In determining how much money is to be paid, a formula for payment must be established. What is this payment for? Payment for unpaid slave labor prior to 1865 is sought. This is a minimum. However, there are reparationists who are not content to stop here. They go on to include payment for *under*paid labor since emancipation.

A third category would include compensation for all of the opportunities denied blacks but which were available to whites. Finally, there is the idea of paying for the cruelty, brutality, degradation, disrupted family life, loss of freedom, enforced ignorance, and disenfranchisement experienced from the beginning of slavery in the U.S. until this present moment.

It is not clear how a figure is determined. Who can calculate the cost in terms of dollars and cents? Who can determine levels of suffering and attach a price to them? Robinson recognizes that material compensation alone can never adequately repay the victims of "great human rights crimes" (224). However, his emphatic and repeated demand for reparation is not congruent with his stated awareness that reparation is not a cure-all.

SOME BIBLICAL CONCEPTS OF POVERTY

Research reveals that the word *poor* often points to one's relationship with God. It may refer to one who is humble, meek, in need of divine deliverance; or to one who is physically weak, afflicted, of low social status. Our definition of *poor* in this study deals with economic deprivation.

What does the Bible have to say about poverty? In very strong language the Bible condemns that poverty which is born of man's own folly. There is a deserved poverty for which we have only ourselves to blame. The Book of Proverbs cautions:

"*He who has a slack hand becomes poor*" (10.4a) "*So shall your poverty come like a prowler*" (24.34; this verse speaks of sleepyheads) "*But he who follows frivolity will have poverty enough*" (28.19) "*Poverty and shame will come to him who disdains correction*" (13.18).

Our hearts go out to those who get caught up in weaknesses that are responsible for such self-induced poverty. Some people are poor because they *Love Pleasure*. The apostle Paul predicted men would be "lovers of pleasure rather than lovers of God" (2 Timothy 3.4). "He who loves pleasure will be a poor man" (Proverbs 21.17a). Some are impoverished by their *Love of Liquor and Luxury*. "He who loves wine and oil will not be rich" (Proverbs 21.17b). Some people are poor because they are *Lazy* (Proverbs 10.4a; 6.6-11). Then there are those whose *Lusts* impoverish them. They are gamblers, covetous chipmunks, lottery lovers, patrons of Saint Bingo. But easy-come money is also easy-go (Jeremiah 17.11).

Furthermore, the greed of some men leads them to take what others possess, thus impoverishing them through swindles, fraud, pigeon-drops, scams, flim-flams, deceit, burglary, embezzlement, robbery, etc. The Bible teaches God is concerned about the poor. Indeed, "The Lord makes poor and makes rich"(1 Samuel 2.7). This fact is repeated in Proverbs 22.2: "The rich and the poor have this in common, the Lord is the maker of them all." "Nor does He regard the rich more than the poor; for they are all the work of His hands" (Job 34.19). This is why the Lord said to the Israelites: "For the poor will never cease from the land" (Deuteronomy 15.11); and Christ said, "For you have the poor with you always, but Me you do not have always" (Matthew 26.11).

We are thus taught that poverty will exist in spite of all of man's efforts to abolish it. Whereas it may not be the goal of the reparationists to eliminate poverty, this biblical message casts absolute doubt on reparation being of any permanent, widespread financial or economic benefit. Human nature being what it is (sinful), money cannot help ease the disproportionate degree of poverty still afflicting American blacks.

SOME SUGGESTED AMOUNTS

I purposely put the following suggested amounts in haphazard order to show the diversity of opinion and estimates. And you will note that "the claims are very flexible" (Barkan, 289). The list suggests (it is not by any means exhaustive) the impossibility of agreeing on an amount that would satisfy everyone, and not later be regretted or revised:

$448 to $995 billion - Jim Marketti

$400 billion and five Southern States: Louisiana, Mississippi, Alabama, Georgia, and South Carolina - Republic of New Africa, a group of 500 black activists organized in 1968; (Marketti sets the capital value of these five states at $350 billion).

$4.1 trillion, plus inflation and interest, owed for labor between 1619 and 1865 - J. Kunjufu.

$50,000 per family of four - Charles Krauthammer: (an expensive amount, but not as costly as the "corruptive alternative of Affirmative Action"; a lump sum will not make full amends for "the debt of the past." In *Time Magazine,* 31 Dec 1990, 18, he suggests $100,000 cash per black family).

$24 trillion - Jack E. White: Though he believes the reparations fight is just, thinks it is a waste of time, and is a totally hopeless cause (*Time Magazine,* 2 Apr 2001, 48).

$8 trillion - And be exempted from income taxes in perpetuity: N'COBRA (National Coalition of Blacks for Reparations in America). For changes see Barkan (383n8).

$3 billion, raised from original demand for $500 million - Black Manifesto, James Forman; also calls for the churches to contribution $15 per black.

$198,149, the value of 40 acres and a mule in 1865, plus the interest that would have accrued over the past - A Tacoma, Washington activist.

$3.4 billion, the value of unpaid income, but "the present value of that exploitation would be over $17 billion" - Roger Ransom and Richard Sutch.

$500,000 - Legal activist, Robert Brock

$300,000 to $400,000 per household - Richard America (33)

$6.6 billion every year for ten years - Reverend Alfred Sharpton's *Black Agenda* (Munford, 420, 429).

"David Swinton concludes that it would take more than the entire wealth of the whole United States to compensate Black folks fully" ... "...the African National Reparations Organization, for one example, is bolder and closer to the mark. It has figured a *minimum* of $4.1 trillion for unpaid labor alone owing just to Black people born within the borders of the United States" (Munford, 429). "The amount we are owed is in the trillions of dollars," is the less precise comment of black nationalist, Haki Madhubuti.

There are those who feel that nothing should be given to black American descendants of slaves. In fact, some have expressed the belief that *welfare* has been an adequate compensation as a matter of justice, and not of charity (Magnet, 133). Twenty-first century Americans feel no responsibility for what happened (or happens) to blacks. "The majority whites simply reject personal responsibility for the living conditions of blacks and thus reject the demand for reparations" (Schuchter, 50).

From a biblical perspective, giving money without a real change of heart on the part of the donor is spiritually unacceptable. If the giver of the *gelt* feels no guilt, he has no need to atone for anything--not a penny, if there is no penitence! Furthermore, there are those of us who believe the demand smacks of bowing down to Our Father Who Art in Washington, a playing up to paternalism. We even feel that it is insulting to think we can be bought.

It is a mistake to assume that money can solve the sin problem. The truth is, no amount of finance or fortitude can undo the tragic results of slavery. And I do not mean to blame all of our ills upon slavery, lest I am counted with the reparationists who have fallen into this very trap. Snap-of-the-finger reparation will not resolve the economic and social disparities, or erase the pain caused by the psychological gap between blacks and whites in this country.

Thomas Sowell (218, 219) rightly challenges the reparationist to prove the present economy of the United States benefited from the slavery of yesteryear. What if it turns out that we are actually "worse off economically because of the historical existence of slavery"? It is impossible to put the black community in an economic position it would have had if there had been no slavery and no discrimination in the United States.

WAYS OF DISBURSEMENT

The question now comes, how should we spend this money? Perhaps better put, how should the reparation debt be paid? This pragmatic question immediately presents us with more knotty problems concerning the issue of reparation to black Americans. The answers are varied and many, indicating also the complexity of the problem.

One answer that seems most acceptable is *not* to give funds to individual blacks. Make no per capita payment directly. Even Congressman John Conyers states, "People seem to me to be moving away from the position of financial remuneration."

Consider first the idea of using the money for relocation or repatriation. Two ideas are suggested here. One is to have blacks leave America, preferably to Africa, and there establish a new home. With his *Universal Negro Improvement Association*, Marcus Garvey hoped to remove millions of blacks from America to Africa. There are whites today who would approve such a transportation. I still have in my possession notes telling me to "Go Home N....." They were slipped in my mail slot in the home we bought, breaking a previously all white block (5721 Chew Ave.).

Garvey did not want integration or reparation! Critics call his stance "reverse racism" (Roy Wilkins, "Integration," *Ebony Magazine*, Aug 1970, 55). Samuel DeWitte Proctor called the black separationists' relocation desire "more a mood, a feeling, than a well-thought out strategy." He said we have no moral basis for trying to separate "from the society in which our forefathers invested so much. We cannot undo the past four hundred years and divest ourselves of all the cultural accretions we have absorbed and invented" (160,170). He calls it "reverse discrimination" (176).

A second idea for relocation involves remaining in North America. The Republic of New Africa has demanded that five Southern states be given over as partial payment: Louisiana, Mississippi, Alabama, Georgia, and South Carolina. Elijah Muhammad also demanded land and provisions so that blacks could establish a separate state or territory -- either on the continent of North America, or elsewhere. He stated that whites (our former slave masters) were obligated to support this venture for the next 20 or 25 years until we become self-supporting.

"Since we cannot get along with them [whites] in peace and equality after giving them 400 years of our sweat and blood and receiving in return some of the worst treatment human beings have ever experienced, we believe our contributions to this land and the suffering forced upon us by white America justifies our demand for complete separation in a state or territory of our own" (*Muhammad,* 38, 161).

We see again the matter of relocation in this paragraph from Malcolm X:

"The Honorable Elijah Muhammad teaches that for the black man in America the only solution is complete *separation* from the white man! ... that since Western society is deteriorating, it has become overrun with immorality, and God is going to judge it, and destroy it. And the only way the black people caught up in this society can be saved is not to *integrate* into this corrupt society, but to *separate* from it, to a land of our *own*, where we can reform ourselves, lift up our moral standards, and try to be godly" (*Autobiography*, 246).

Second, there is the proposal to remain where we are, and use the money in various other ways, establishing trust funds, grants, and investments. Corporate entities would handle the distribution of reparation payments. However, who would be the members of these corporations? Who would pick them? Or has the white man done this for us already? Have existing black organizations, churches, fraternal orders, reform groups, or revolutionary committees made themselves the leaders? Have black magazine publishers, newspaper editors, mayors and government officials set themselves as chief executives? Alternatively, as Bittker (81) adds, are poets, performers, intellectuals, civil servants, and other "unaffiliated notables," self-appointed leaders?

SUGGESTED USE OF THE FUNDS

Ideas offered for the use of reparation funds include:

(1) Develop various community projects
(2) Provide college scholarships for needy black students, and do whatever else it takes to eliminate the black education gap, even vouchers
(3) Revitalize impoverished inner city neighborhoods
(4) Make business loans to black entrepreneurs
(5) Battle AIDS
(6) Do something about the high incarceration rate of blacks
(7) Provide health care: sickle cell anemia, diabetes, colon cancer, hypertension, infant mortality rates, other afflictions prevailing among blacks
(8) Housing
(9) Job opportunities and job training
(10) Step up Affirmative Action
(11) Crime prevention efforts

SOME CRITICISMS

Several criticisms come to mind immediately. One: Too much weight is put upon human efforts (without Christ) to overcome immorality. We are blind to the spiritual forces operating and causing changes that take place in our society. There is the failure to see that God has not left it up to man to make the world a better place in which to live. All too often men are carried away with their schemes -- their Great Society, Utopia, War on Poverty -- and by leaving God out, are doomed to failure.

Two: The desire to place blacks in the financial position believed would exist if slavery had never occurred is unrealistic. What position is this? (D'Souza, 67,68). Is it the same position white Americans are in? Which whites? Sowell (218-219) stated,

"If the purpose of reparations is to share equitably the economic contributions of slavery to the present economy, then it would first be necessary to establish that there were in fact net benefits. If the country is in set balance worse off economically because of the historical existence of slavery on its soil, then there are no benefits to share, equitably or otherwise."

FORTY ACRES AND A MULE

Four million highly visible blacks, nearly all illiterate, totally unorganized, were let loose to wander, penniless, propertyless, in a war-torn, economically deprived and racially hostile area. Many of these freedmen held that restitution should be made for their years of unpaid labor, and they expected the Federal Government to provide them with farm land so they could settle down as independent farmers.[1]

On January 12, 1865, Union General William T. Sherman, along with Secretary of War Edwin Stanton, met in Savannah, Georgia, with twenty black preachers and church officers, believing that ownership of land was the key to a successful transition from slavery to freedom. There are still those today who believe that if each slave family had gotten 40 acres and a mule, that race relations in America today would be completely different.

General Sherman issued Special Field Order No.15 some days after this meeting. The order granted "possession titles" to forty-acre lots of land situated on a 30-mile stretch of the low-country rice coast between Charleston, South Carolina, and Jacksonville, Florida. Southerner owners had abandoned this land. It was not Sherman's plan for a long term commitment, "but rather temporary military expedients, designed to keep them working on the plantations and away from the cities and the Union Army camps" (Litwack, 404).

The newly established Freedmen's Bureau, created in March, 1865 to help the blacks, became the custodian of all abandoned and confiscated property. The hopes of the freedmen were high, for they believed owning their own land confirmed their emancipation.

However, it was not to be. For one thing, it still was not clear whether the Federal Government held legal title to Southern land. Second, the black skin of the freed slaves did not prevent them from experiencing the same problems that plagued many white farmers. Third, there were whites who did all they could to defraud those blacks who held legitimate title to lands. Fourth, on May 29, 1865, President Andrew Johnson pardoned most former Confederates and their land was restored to them. Thus the hope of receiving the "forty acres" collapsed.

Thaddeus Stevens, a wealthy Pennsylvania lawyer who became a congressman, and Charles Sumner, and others belonging to what came to be called Radical or Congressional Reconstruction, attempted to send through a bill maintaining what General Sherman had done earlier. However, President Johnson vetoed it.

Then in July 1866, the Southern Homestead Act was passed as Congress tried again to ratify distribution of land. This too failed. By the middle of 1867, the Radical Republican congressmen gave up concentrating on redistribution of land to the former slaves; instead they turned their attention to securing the right of blacks to vote.

However, former slaveholders were allowed to disenfranchise the blacks, effectively removing them from any meaningful participation in public life. All kinds of stumbling blocks were put in their way. You can see how the expression "forty acres and a mule" came to be used by black Americans to symbolize empty promises, a debt unpaid.

Forty acres and a mule have been calculated presently to be worth $198,149 (A.Asadullah Samad, A7). L.G. Sherrod (*Essence Magazine*) advocated black Americans should file for a $43,209 tax rebate. According to her figures this was the current equivalent of the "forty acres and a mule," calculated by subtracting the 1990 census figures of the median wealth of the black household from that of the white household ($4,606 subtracted from $47,815).

Du Bois (602) said: "To have given each one of the million

Negro families a forty-acre freehold would have made a basis of real democracy in the United States that might easily have transformed the modern world." Commenting on Du Bois' statement, Myrdahl says, "This may be true enough, but it should be kept clear that the historical setting would hardly have allowed it ... the white South was ... for the most part violently against any constructive program framed to raise the Negro freedmen to economic independence" (224, 226). Human nature being what it is, it is highly doubtful race relations in the U.S. would be any better if blacks had received the forty acres and the mule.[2]

CHAPTER 6 -WHO PAYS AND WHO RECEIVES?

It is difficult, nay, impossible to separate the categories, who pays and who receives reparation. This is because some contemporary black Americans are descendants of slave traders, some are offspring of slave owners, and some are descendants of Africans who sold Africans into bondage. There are also blacks in the U.S. who are recent immigrants from various African, Caribbean and South American countries.[1]

The difficulty is compounded by the fact that some contemporary *white* Americans are distant blood relatives of blacks, descendants of slave owners, slave traders, families that never owned slaves, etc. And of course, there is the recent influx of people from Asia, and the rapidly increasing numbers of Hispanics. Nonetheless, we seek in this chapter to point out the problems associated with determining who should be the recipients of reparation, as well as the problem associated with deciding who should pay the reparation.

1. Consider first those **Africans Who Sold Africans into Slavery:** As grievous as it is to black reparationists, it is a fact that Africans sold Africans into slavery. Strangely, some black reparationists have little to say about this (for example, Munford, 413-439). Perhaps it detracts from their so-called "morale boosting" glorification of the African past. Slavery has been a worldwide institution for centuries, among the most disparate races and cultures. African slavery was both widespread and uncontroversial.

"Europeans did not possess the military power to force Africans to participate in any type of trade in which their leaders did not wish to engage. Therefore all African trade with the Atlantic, including the slave trade, had to be voluntary" (Thornton, 7). American blacks unaware of the part played by Africans in the African slave trade may be disillusioned to discover this truth, and even unwilling to accept it.

In her book, *Dust Tracks on a Road* (242), Zora Neale Hurston writes about her dismay upon learning the role played by Africans. Although whites bought and exploited slaves, black Africans sold black Africans to the whites. Hurston reminded me of how often we joke among ourselves about our foibles, but I had never heard before the self-deprecating piece of folklore in which it is stated the white man waved a red flag in front of the Africans, and enticed them into the ships that carried them away.

The author states she was devastated to learn the results of the love of money. She was sobered by the realization that it is historically true that her "own people had butchered and killed, exterminated whole nations and torn families apart, for a profit before the strangers got their chance at a cut." Hurston admitted something many reparationists seem unwilling to concede: All humans are afflicted with "the universal nature of greed and glory."

Whites did not just invade the continent, chase and capture slaves. African kingdoms such as Dahomey, Ashanti, Sierra Leone, Gambia, and the Congo were already engaged in the slave trade, perpetuated by warfare and kidnapping. Therefore it was no strange thing to sell slaves to the white man. The African coastal chiefs successfully restrained Europeans who sought to penetrate the interior to obtain slaves. Africans also fought each other to maintain their position (Davidson, 86). You can see why critics of reparation say it is politically hypocritical to demand redress from the West while making no such demand from the Africans or the Muslims. Whereas Europeans considered land their primary source of wealth, Africans recognized slaves as their only form of private, revenue-producing property (Thornton, 73-76, 95).

It is concluded by Thornton (125), that "we must accept that African participation in the slave trade was voluntary and under the control of African decision makers. This was not just at the surface level of daily exchange but even at deeper levels. Europeans possessed no means, either economic or military, to compel African leaders to sell slaves."

The question comes, "Should the descendants of Africans who

sold Africans into slavery be made to pay reparation to the descendants of black American slaves?" Who determines who and where these progeny of African slave traders are found today?

2. **Europeans Who Sold Africans into Slavery:** For some 250 years Europeans engaged in the African slave trade, and exacerbated their evil by remapping and carving up the African continent for further economic exploitation. At one time the following countries had colonies in Africa: Britain, France, Belgium, Italy, Germany, Portugal, Spain.

Many books on the African slave trade reveal the roles played by these nations. Though many names of individuals are listed in these books, who can track down the offspring of these European slave traders, in view of the fact several centuries have elapsed?

Even though Europeans for the most part did not invade Africa and capture slaves, they are guilty of promoting the slave trade through indirect military technology. Through the Europeans, Africans were able to purchase guns to defend themselves, and to successfully wage war against their African enemies and obtain more slaves. This is what is meant by European influence by "means of destruction," indirectly affecting the slave trade. Yet with their "fire power" the whites were unable to make Africans participate in any kind of trade if the African leaders refused to do so. African slave trade then had to be voluntary (Thornton, 7).

3. **White Union Army Soldiers:** Why should the descendants of these soldiers pay reparation when they were instrumental in freeing the slaves? True, they fought in the war, but one suspects that very few white Union soldiers gave this reason any priority.

4. **Indians (Native Americans) Who Owned African Slaves:** Choctaws, Chickasaws, Cherokees, Creeks and Seminoles are some of the tribes that owned black slaves (Bennett, 100, 300). Though the numbers held by Native Americans were small compared to the numbers held by the whites, the fact that Native Americans held slaves at all further complicates the matter of who qualifies to receive reparation, and who should give it.

5. **Poor Whites Who Owned No Slaves:** Should the descendants of poor whites who owned no slaves file for reparation? After all, it is impossible to keep down blacks without at the same time adversely affecting whites. So that there were whites who kept their feet on the necks of other whites. The greed for money and the lust for power are color blind! Poor whites justly claim that the enslavement of blacks also caused hardships to them.[2]

6. **Should Well-Off Black Americans Receive Anything?:** J. Kunjufu (30) states: "Individual success stories of African Americans becoming millionaires cannot negate the large numbers that live below the poverty level..." However would blacks living beneath the poverty level approve of rich blacks accepting such funds? I think not. It may well be that these wealthy blacks would not accept such money, but would request it be turned over to some special fund.

Perhaps we should ask Bill Cosby, Oprah Winfrey, Michael Jordan, Kobe Bryant, Michael Jackson, Denzel Washington, Tiger Woods, Allen Iverson, Shaquille O'Neal, Linda Johnson Rice, Spike Lee, Wesley Snipes; or even Randall Robinson ("lucky petit bourgeois"), who does not appear to be in financial need! Barkan (292, 293) states that middle-class blacks consider the demand for reparation a "counterproductive preoccupation," and that they would reject any discussion of restitution as perpetuating a "victim complex" that distracts them from finding true solutions to their problems. Horowitz states that all this push for reparation does is "inflate the victim mentality in the black community, which is the main thing that's still holding black people down."

Add then to the complication of deciding who gets what, the names of those blacks who insist, "I don't want it-- no reparation money for me!" As Bayard Rustin said, "If my great-grandfather picked cotton for 50 years, then he may deserve some money, but he's dead and nobody owes me anything" (*New York Times,* 9 May 1969, 44).

7. **White Abolitionists**: Should the descendants of white abolitionists and others who fought against slavery be made to contribute to the reparation fund? For it is a fact that some American whites vehemently opposed black slavery, and some of them paid dearly for their opposition. A white roofer from Durham, New Hampshire, said: "My family supported the Underground Railroad. Why should I have to pay?" One hostile white is reported to have said, "You should pay reparations to the ancestors of Union troops who died to secure your freedom. My great grandfather being one of them. So send me your checks today!"

8. **Muslims Who Sold Africans into Slavery:** Working through Arab middlemen, African tribal chiefs and tribes became rich supplying the Europeans with millions of slaves (D'Souza, 73).

Sowell (189) writes:

"It was only the fact that the slave trade to the Islamic countries began earlier and continued longer that made the Middle East and North Africa the largest absorber of black Africans as slaves over the centuries. Moreover, it is only the existence of a vastly greater literature on slavery in the Western world than in the Islamic world which creates the myopic illusion that slavery, or even African slavery, was a predominantly European phenomenon."

Arab slave trade covered many centuries: 652 A.D. (Arab-Nubian Slave Treaty) until 1890, actually ending in 1911. "It was the Arabs who set the foundations for exporting Africans, for taking the people of Africa to strange and horrible lands" (Anderson, 34). It is estimated that at least 9.64 million African women and 4.75 million African men were sold in the Arab Slave Trade.

From 14 to 20 million Africans were slain while resisting capture or en route to be sold, "waiting to board the slave ships or caravans bound for the Muslim world, at the holding pens and dungeons ... or in the process of being castrated for eunuch slavedom" (Anderson, 41).

Here again is a formidable, if not impossible task. Who can trace the descendants of the Islamic slave traders of yesteryear? Obtaining slaves from East Africa was a major Arab enterprise after 1840. We have trouble even now seeking to stamp out slavery practiced by certain Islamic countries this very day! What success would we have in apprehending the children of Arab sea captains and merchants, slave traders and their backers? Far too many American blacks *gung ho* on joining Islam apparently are unaware of the part played by Arabs in African slavery.

Nor are they aware of the ongoing slave trade presently perpetrated by Muslims in the Sudan. Calling Christianity "the white man's religion" while ignoring the historical role played by Islam in the black African slave trade, and refusing to study the living conditions in those countries ruled by Islam, black Americans reject the claims of Jesus Christ and join Islam. They face a dark future, a hopeless eternity.

9. Blacks in America Who Owned Slaves: Wouldn't it be ironic if it were discovered that the ancestors of some reparationists were blacks who owned slaves? That there were thousands of black slave owners in America is indisputable (D'Souza, 71, 75-77). In 1830 there were more than 3,500 (3,777: Munford, 214) American black slave owners who collectively owned more than 10,000 black slaves.

Prior to Emancipation in 1865, approximately 14 percent of the blacks in the United States were free. Of this approximate half million there existed a considerable number who owned slaves themselves. Just as the majority of white slave owners lived in Louisiana, South Carolina, Maryland and Virginia, so practically all of the black proprietors were in the South. Louisiana and Old Dominion Virginia housed most of them (Munford, 214).

However, there were black slave owners in the North, for at the time some whites up North owned slaves, and there were blacks who followed in their footsteps. Numerically, free blacks were almost evenly split between North and South; in time, of course, their numbers in the Deep South declined (Sowell, 198).

Now it should be noted that the census records indicate most of the blacks who owned slaves were philanthropists. Husbands purchased wives (or vice versa); or the slaves were children of a free father but born to a slave mother. Slaves purchased by free blacks were later granted freedom for a nominal sum of money or liberal work agreement (Woodson, v-vii).

How extensive then was black slave holding in the American South? Compared with the number of slaves owned by whites, black holdings were not extensive. Yet the numbers held are enough to be morally disturbing (D'Souza, 78). Assuming we find the descendants of black slave owners, how should the black reparationists deal with them? Should we erase their names as recipients of reparation? Should we make them pay? What happens if they file suit against the reparationists?

Suppose, suppose! You would think there are enough suppositions already inherent in the case against reparation to cause the proponents to see the futility of their cause.

Recognizing the truth black slave owners existed, Munford (214) grouses, "These abettors of their own people's disgrace grounded a tradition still sadly with us in the form of Black neo-conservatives securely niched today in posts everywhere from the Supreme Court to the armed services to the nation's universities and board-rooms."[3]

WHO IS AN AFRICAN AMERICAN?

Is there a percentage of "black blood" that qualifies one to receive reparation? How do light-skinned blacks fit in? Should they receive a lesser reparation? Can we ignore the "color thing" and the "class thing"? "For generations of black people, color and caste have been inexorably tied together" (Graham, 49).[4]

"There has been enough mating across racial lines in the United States to justify the prediction that hundreds of thousands, if not millions, of persons of debatable racial composition might apply for compensation if the benefits were worth pursuing. It has been estimated that over thirty-six million Americans classified as white in 1960 had 'an African element in their inherited biological background.' This means that the Africans brought to the United States have more 'white' than 'black' descendants" (Bittker, 95,96).

Because of blood ties some blacks received favored status. Work inside the homes of the whites as butlers, maids, mammies, they had more interaction with the whites. There was more opportunity to learn to read. And there were more light-skinned free blacks than there were dark-skinned free blacks.

PASSING

"Passing" is the word used of one who has "Negro blood" but whose skin color is fair and features are not Negroid, and who is accepted as or believed to be white. The term is used informally of Negroes; it means to be accepted as white (*World Book Dictionary, pass*). *"...numerous persons with only a few Negroid traits annually 'pass over' and are absorbed into the dominant caucasoid population"* (Beals & Hoijer, *World Book Dictionary*). "To live or be known as a member of a racial, religious, or ethnic group other than one's own, especially to live and be known as a white person although of black ancestry" (*Random House Unabridged Dictionary, CD-Rom*). Gunnar Myrdahl concludes: "It is difficult to determine the extent of passing...the backwash of miscegenation, and one of its surest results" (129). Here then is one more piece of the problem we face in determining reparation. As someone has suggested, "These issues could produce a lively trade for genealogists, DNA testers, and other such quacks!"

Even if we could make certain who are the children of all the slave traders and slave owners, the matter of gathering them together and prosecuting them is unlikely. It is obvious that this is a very complex matter. There is also the moral and legal issue of the rightness or wrongness of seeking payment from the descendants of all who were involved in the black African slave trade. Are slave traders as guilty as slave owners? In addition, of what are their descendants guilty?

Summary: The more we think about it, the more we realize the impossibility of determining who should pay and who should receive remuneration. Discovering who held what **Position**: slave-trader, slave owner, slave master, slave, butler, field hand, free blacks, investor, Union soldier, Confederate soldier; **Race or Nationality:** Native American, Caucasian, African, Arab, immigrant (before or after the Civil War); **Relationship:** husband, wife, mistress, unmarried mother or father, children born out of wedlock, disrupted family, etc.; **Economic Condition**: rich, poor, middle-class, etc. Mix these various factors and you will come up with all kinds of combinations. There are those who could wish for a simpler process, perhaps just skin color. But even this would not guarantee who should or should not accept or give reparation.

CHAPTER 7 - THE ROLE OF HUMANISM IN THE DEMAND FOR BLACK REPARATION

There is no human solution for the racial climate produced in the United States by nearly two hundred and fifty years of slavery (1619-1865), followed by more than one hundred and thirty-five years of segregation, Jim Crow, and bigotry (1866-present). Theonomists (Reconstructionists, post-millennialists) and others, call this point of view defeatism, pessimistic eschatology. However, to believe that it is up to man to make the world a better place in which to live is neither Scriptural nor realistic.

Today's news does not support the optimism held that we can solve racial difficulties. The headlines supply no such encouragement. Black unemployment, housing restrictions, unequal educational facilities, poor health care services, prejudiced media, legal maneuvering calculated to maintain white supremacy, unequal job opportunities, police brutality, a biased criminal justice system, voting fraud, and racist religious institutions -- still plague us! Racism is demonic.

And the demons of racial discrimination are not exorcised by reparation, affirmative action, or legislation. To believe otherwise indicates naivete or ignorance born either of the failure to accept the biblical concept of man's makeup, or a deliberate rejection of the Bible as the Word of God.

HUMANISM DEFINED

What is humanism? It is a way of looking at life and the world through anthropocentric eyes; it puts man at the very center of all things, while leaving God out of all deliberations. This particular brand of humanism, perhaps better called **Secular Humanism** (Lockerbie, 196), feels that God is not needed. Humanism often rejects the importance of belief in God (Random House Dictionary).Humanism usually refuses to accept supernaturalism (Encyclopedia Britannica Dictionary). "Man is considered to be his own god, and thus the maker of his own rules, standards, and value systems" (Jackson, 302). The humanist's favorite poem is *Invictus,* by William Ernest Henley:

"Out of the night that covers me,
    Black as the Pit from pole to pole,
I thank whatever gods may be
    For my unconquerable soul.
In the fell clutch of circumstance
    I have not winced nor cried aloud.
Under the bludgeonings of chance
    My head is bloody, but unbowed.
Beyond this place of wrath and tears
    Looms but the Horror of the shade,
And yet the menace of the years
    Finds, and shall find, me unafraid.
It matters not how strait the gate,
    How charged with punishments the scroll,
I am the master of my fate:
    I am the captain of my soul."

HUMANISM DENIES BIBLICAL CONCEPTS

Humanists deny the sinful nature of humanity (*World Book Encyclopedia*). They reject the Bible teaching that sin resides in the hearts of all people (Jeremiah 17.9; Mark 7.21-23; Romans 3.23). How sin manifests itself depends on many factors: opportunity, tradition, environment, customs, circumstances, ability, education, climate, economics, etc.

It is a mistake to ignore the value of the spiritual aspect of life. Man is not a mere animal. If we seek only the profit or well-being of the outer man and fail to nurture the inner person, our lost souls remain lost, out of fellowship with God. Our impression of Randall Robinson is that of a lost soul. Humanism is at the very core of his philosophy of life. He confesses in his book, *The Debt*, he does not attend church (58). His vain use of the name of Jesus Christ (31) and foul language (207, 217) do not speak well of his spiritual condition.

This is not to say that all supporters of black reparation are going to Hell; nor is it to say that all who resist the movement are going to Heaven. Believers and unbelievers, blacks and whites, are found in both the pro and con camps of black reparation. What we suggest is that Robinson's disregard for the church and the Bible has colored his outlook on life.

Charles Krauthammer, (*Time Magazine*, 31 Dec 1990, p 18), expresses well this humanism that so typically overlooks the matter of the sinful heart:

"It is time to reclaim the notion of color blindness before it is too late. A one-time reparation to blacks would help real people in a real way. It would honor our obligation to right ancient wrongs. And it would allow us all a new start. America could then rededicate itself to Martin Luther King Jr.'s proposition that Americans be judged by the content of their character, not by the color of their skin."

Munford (401) speaks of certain religious beliefs that build self-confidence, that "give a sense of worthiness in the day-to-day struggle for Black liberation." He cites the religious beliefs (does not tell what they are) that inspired "Black Southerners fighting for civil rights ... Malcolm X's belief in Allah ... Voodoo tradition ..." It is evident he knows little about the power of Christ, as he opines (537):

"...admonishing folks to be good has never worked. Not once in the entire history of the human race. Ethical upbringing has severe limitations as the catalyst of real social transformation. The time has come to offer our people a less exalted alternative, a 'less' moral and spiritual precept, but one with more potential clout. I would have us seek *power*."

LEGALISM IS ALSO AN ASPECT OF HUMANISM

I have said little about the legal battle involved in the demand for reparation. Lawyers, and legislators will surely take me to task for not having more to say about their work regarding reparation. The legal aspect is another complicated phase of the problem of reparation (statute of limitations, defining damage, sovereign immunity, countersuits, class-certification, etc.).[1] Those interested should see Forum: "Making the Case for Racial Reparations." *Harper's Magazine*, Nov 2000. Four of the country's most successful class-action lawyers were invited to strategize about how to bring "America's most peculiar sorrow into a court of law."

Legalism is also an aspect of humanism. It is the belief that passing laws will solve our ills. However, men are often unaware that some things declared legal are immoral (abortion, gambling, prostitution, slavery, etc.). As a Christian I have an obligation to obey the law, so long as that law does not violate my right to worship God, in which case I offer Caesar what is his, but give unto the Lord what is His (Matthew 22.21). Understand that whatever Caesar has, God gave or allowed him to have it.

If the law permits slavery, I cannot sue the government if later that law is changed. The people made the law and abided by it. They should not now be penalized (their descendants should not) for obeying a law that has now been changed or abolished. As a Christian I should strive to be led of the Holy Spirit when it comes to practicing that which may be permissible by law.

John Myers, State Representative (Pa.), reintroduced legislation to establish a commission to study the long-term effects of slavery in Pennsylvania and the twelve other original colonies. He said, "I look on this bill as a catalyst for a national soul-searching, airing it out and coming clean on slavery and the impact of lingering racism" (*The Leader*, 30 May 2001).

Bittker (127) admits that even if a judicial decision upholding the constitutionality of black reparation is made, the dangers are substantial, the problems many, the implementation colossal. He admits that "money alone will not 'cure' all the problems, diseases, deficiencies, etc" (129).

Reading Richard America's *Paying the Social Debt: What White America Owes Black America* led me to characterize his work with the words, "God is in none of his thoughts" (Psa 10.4). It reeks with humanism! Boris Bittker's *The Case for Black Reparations* is also very strong on legal actions taken to remedy "injuries caused by a system of legally imposed segregation" (19).

He considers the racial discrimination practiced "against blacks was systematic, unrelenting, authorized at the highest govern-mental levels, and practiced by large segments of the population" and that injuries suffered under "a legal system held to violate the Constitution ... institutionalized deprivation of a group's constitutional rights" should be legally redressed (21-24). However, I would point out that black slaves were not citizens!

An editorial that appeared in *The Philadelphia Inquirer*, 20 May 2001, reminds us of the role that may be played by a team of lawyers constituting the Reparation Coordinating Committee.

Johnnie Cochran, Charles J. Ogletree, Alexander J. Pires, Jr.,

Randall Robinson, and Richard F. Scruggs are included in this Committee. Because in the past the courts have played a large part in the desegregation and integration efforts of blacks in the nation, many reparationists feel that only lawsuits can advance their cause.

We agree with the Inquirer article that although lawsuits may further justice, they are not formulated to create healing. It is our opinion that black reparation is a moral issue, and therefore it is impossible to achieve healing through any legal means. Healing comes only with a change of heart.

You see then the role given to the legal aspect of black reparation. Lillian Swanson, assistant managing editor/ombudsman told how the newspaper reached the decision to print editorials on reparations *(The Philadelphia Inquirer*, 28 May 2001). The editorial called for a national or Congressional dialogue, in which by acknowledging the facts of the evils of black slavery, the government could take steps to make amends, and produce reconciliation between the races. Our response: This is vintage humanism to think that "acknowledgment" will produce "atonement," and "reconciliation.".

TOO MUCH WEIGHT PUT UPON REPARATION

The black reparationist expects to accomplish too much through reparation; he puts too much weight on black reparation. For example, N'COBRA (National Coalition of Blacks for Reparations in America) believes that reparation is "the first step in the healing process and is necessary to repair for previous injustices. The effects of slavery, Jim Crow and institutional racism still exist. Reparations is one means of supporting a sick community so that it can heal itself of America's atrocities." This is a pipe dream; it is manifest ignorance of the depth of man's sin nature and man's woeful, inadequate ability to deal with sin successfully. The weight put upon black reparation results in a false optimism. For example, Randall Robinson told *Time*'s Elaine Rivera, "I don't think among rational people that you can argue that a graver crime has occurred than slavery ... Whites will come to recognize for moral and practical reasons that reparations benefit the whole of society." To this statement, Jack White responded, "He has a lot more faith in human nature than I do."

Although Robinson states affirmative action will never even come close to solving our problems (8, 9), He goes on to claim that it is impossible for the United States to solve its racial problems if its black citizens are not compensated for governmental exploitation inflicted during and after slavery. It is a mistake to put this much weight on reparation. Yet Robinson insists that the demand for reparation would begin a "healing of our psyches ... make us more forgiving of ourselves, more self-approving, more self-understanding" (208). This is pure psychobabble!

We see in the words of Samuel Proctor (96) another example of thinking too highly of the effect of black reparation., Proctor claims there are blacks who "enjoyed an education and job placement that would never have occurred without the steady protest and advocacy of black agitators."

He makes a mistake I find common among the social gospel, humanist crowd. They drop an unbearable load upon human efforts to overcome immorality. Evidently, they are blind to the spiritual forces operating and forcing the changes that take place in our society. They overlook the achievements made by blacks *without* the efforts of "black agitators." And fail to see that the time was ripe for social upheavals. They suggest the changes came *sooner* with their methods, rather than *later* with the methods of the passive, peace at any cost blacks.

"There can be no 'color-blind' society **without** affirmative action, minority set-asides, and reparations. These are remedial measures impossible to enact without deliberate government action, and without them, ancient wrongs will never be redressed, new racial parities will never see (the) light of day" (Munford, 534, 535).

Munford also predicts: "Should we fail to win reparations, we will have lost the war forever, there will be nothing left for North American Blacks but gradual extinction in the course of the next century or two" (436). I feel nothing but pity for any man who believes this non-biblical trash-talk, this pessimism extraordinaire, born of humanism![2]

HUMANISM AND SELF-ESTEEM

The term "self-esteem" is often on the lips of the secular humanist. He teaches we need reparation to bolster black selfhood, and so he grasps after the straws of yesteryear in order to satisfy a sense of belonging and identification. Robinson and others believe that a deep awareness of our past is necessary for a successful future. Robinson said, "No people can live successfully, fruitfully, triumphantly without strong memory of their past, without reading the future within the context of some reassuring past, without implanting reminders of that past in the present" (27).

This humanist approach fails to move me. It is not that I have no appreciation for the history of various African nations or empires. I learned early that nations rise and fall and civilizations come and go. Knowledge of Africa's past has never impressed me, positively or negatively. Even as an American citizen, I realize that the greatness of this country will not last (Prov. 14.34)..

Now you would think that by looking at what black Americans have accomplished in the very midst of racism, that black reparationists would not be afflicted with a lack of self-esteem. Undeniably, blacks have made great contributions to America (Wachtel, 145-148).

A reading of Ira Berlin's book, *Many Thousands Gone*, reveals the varied skills, tasks and positions of blacks in the very heart of an enforced servitude. Carpenters, millers, shoemakers, blacksmiths, masons, brick makers, hairdressers, machinists, saddlers, wheelwrights, coopers, domestics, coachmen, valets, chimney sweeps, merchant seamen, butchers, bakers, tailors, cigar makers, caulkers, ropemakers, sail makers, hatters, cooks, seamstresses, barbers, caterers, soldiers, boatmen, wagoners, and farmers working with corn, cotton, indigo, rice, sugar, wheat, and tobacco.

From the perspective of our total stay in America, add the following achievers: Preachers, teachers, inventors, athletes (boxing, baseball, basketball, football, tennis, track, golf); missionaries and evangelists, lawyers, doctors, explorers, dentists; musicians (composers, singers, instrumentalists); civil rights leaders, politicians and legislators, government officials, journalists, scientists, business men and women, entertainers (movies, theater, television), etc.

Many reparationists are aware of these accomplishments, yet argue that reparation is needed to build up self-esteem. What moves one black, who knows of these achievements, to turn bitter and demand compensation, while another black, also aware of these accomplishments, makes no such demand, but is motivated to achieve even more? Which approach is beneficial from a biblical point of view, which attitude is moral? Would I dare suggest, "Ask not what America can do for me, but concentrate on what I can do for America"?

I was not born down-South in Philadelphia, Mississippi, but up-South, in Philadelphia, Pennsylvania. My first ride in the back of a segregated bus was when I was stationed in Fort Bragg, NC in an all-black paratrooper outfit (555th), and rode from Fayetteville to Lumberton to see if I could locate the Love family. I never picked cotton, but I did pick trash as a scavenger (junkman) who collected paper, rags, copper wire and returnable soda bottles.

I never saw any "Colored Only" or "White Only" signs, but I had to sit in the balcony of the Liberty Theater in North Philadelphia; only whites were allowed to view the movies from the main floor of the auditorium -- but there were no signs posted! Linton's restaurant would not allow us to sit down in its establishment; we walked all the way through, ordered food, and took it out.

I never heard any white man call me n-----, though it was a word often bandied about in the black community. Instead, the young whites at Northeast High School called me "Tar baby" and "Snowball" --- to which I responded, "Why don't you guys make up your minds!" The swimming pool at the YMCA then located at Lehigh Avenue, near Eleventh Street, refused me admission. I shined shoes (my main source of income as a boy), scrubbed floors, set up pins in bowling alleys (jumping alleys), even while attending the University of Pennsylvania on the G.I. Bill.

What strikes me as ironic is this: ***I don't believe America owes me anything.*** I agree with Sowell (220) that it is a "distortion of history to assume blacks are owed anything" by America. I am not bitter about the countless known and unknown experiences with racism. What does disturb me is what I perceive as a spirit of bitterness in those who speak of America's debt to black descendants of slaves.

I fear that those who demand reparation have let their own brand of racism express itself in biting resentment, the desire for revenge, hatred of whites, and because the bug of materialism bites them, they are blind to the error of their demands.

Take for example the twisted logic, and immoral thinking of Munford (414) which cannot help but exacerbate race relations when he declares that when Blacks commit robbery, larceny, fraud, defacement, vandalism, or such, against white-owned property he "cannot find it in 'his' heart to condemn as a *crime*" any such act. They are "merely recovering values stolen from us as an oppressed and enslaved people ... recovering surplus value created by the unpaid forced labor of their enslaved ancestors ..." Unbelievable!

FAILURE TO PERSEVERE

There is also the gnawing fear that the demand for reparation gives evidence of the loss of that spirit that perseveres in affliction! Magnet (133-134) considers reparation a form of welfare, and states what is considered "a universal truth," namely, "The more subsidies you have, the less self-reliant people will be." Men put too much stock in the mistaken concept of the miracle-working beneficence and healing attributes of reparation.

We have made terrific gains while living in an unequal society. What guarantee is there that we will achieve more if reparation is given? This entire humanist emphasis helps play down or lessen the responsibility, desire and motivation to battle through present-day adversities. It is indeed unfortunate that secular humanism is at the very core of the drive for black compensation to slave descendants.

For the Christian, recovery of stolen history is not nearly as important as knowledge of a certain future with Jesus Christ. Do not dismiss this as mere religious sentiment, or with a glib accusation of sermonizing. After all, I am a Bible Teacher. My faith teaches me that it is immoral to demand payment be given to the descendants of black slavery for the unpaid labor of yesteryear. Two wrongs do not make a right. Moreover it is my faith that moves me with passion against the reparation movement!

Humanist-based reparation will ultimately fail in achieving its goal. We guarantee failure by gliding over cultural contexts, ignoring sin in the human heart -- a heart that expresses itself in the sins of idolatry, superstition, ignorance, tribalism, caste, greed, nationalism and racism. We cannot ignore the impact of such natural calamities as earthquakes, hurricanes, drought, pestilence, disease, unfav-orable climate. These are all factors in creating and maintaining poverty. Realize also there is an evil being called Satan who plays a part in the physical and spiritual impoverishment of mankind. These facts sound the death knell to humanism.

CHAPTER 8 - HERITABILITY

"My family supported the Underground Railroad... "Members of my family were Abolitionists"... "My family never owned any slaves"... "Members of my family fought in the Union Army"... "My great grand daddy helped slaves escape from bondage." These are remarks made by whites with Pre-Emancipation roots in

America. *"I too suffered persecution when I arrived here in 1910"... "We did not cause slavery. We were not alive during the existence of black slavery. So it is not fair to hold us responsible for deeds done before we were born."* These are some of the remarks made by whites with Post-Emancipation roots.

DEFINITION

Heritability is the capability of passing something from one generation to the next. The question comes, is it correct to hold the present generation of white Americans liable for paying reparation to the descendants of black slaves? I am not sure I favor the use of the word, *heritability*. It sounds too much like someone has voluntarily, knowingly left something for me either to enjoy or suffer, thus presenting me with an inadequate description of the results and situations Americans find themselves in today.

Undeniably contemporary whites enjoy the benefits of a society built by those who preceded them. They ride piggy-back on the status quo of discrimination presently practiced in the U.S. One wonders how well off whites would be had they been required to compete with blacks who never suffered the inferiorating practices of injustice, segregation, disfranchisement, exploitation, and woefully inadequate educational facilities![1]

The "patterns of complicity extended throughout U.S. society and still affect each one of us," and there is "an ongoing pattern of individual behavior that is interwoven with predominant social patterns" (Barnett, 1071). This is why reparationists contend that the impact of slavery is pervasively evident right now, and the time period for reparation should be 1619 - 2002 (right now!).

Worrill (*The Philadelphia Tribune,* 24 Apr 2001), cites John Hope Franklin's response to David Horowitz's "Ten Reasons" advertisement. It is pointed out that contemporary Americans certainly have a connection with yesteryear's slavery. Franklin suggests Americans have inherited from slavery either advantages or disadvantages. Some disadvantages are housing segregation, inadequate educational facilities, job discrimination, injustice, low self-esteem, racial profiling ["driving while black"], and a host of other conditions which indicate "the vestiges of slavery are still with us."

In a similar fashion, Sam Proctor (94) also speaks of the "inherited disabilities and stigmas and accrued financial, educational, and social *deficits*" of blacks, and of similarly accrued financial, educational, and power *benefits* of whites. "It is fair for this generation that enjoys those unfair advantages to compensate blacks for such unfairly imposed deficits."

Now what we say of whites is also true of blacks in America. There is no escaping the fact that in spite of all the evils perpetrated against blacks, we too have been blessed by what others have contributed in building America. All countries, all civilizations of every age are built upon the work of others. It cannot be otherwise. So when the question is broached, "Who owes whom what?" and if owed, "How much, and when should it be paid?" We find ourselves in a dilemma.

I do not deny that slavery has created certain deficits for blacks. However, the plus and minus effect is not limited to either group. For a contemporary white American to admit he profits in some degree from the past labor of slavery, and from the present racial situation in America is a realistic assessment. All civilization is built upon the events of history, whether upon injustices or humane acts, war or peace, times of depression or prosperity, etc. Why hold the descendants of such evil guilty?

Admittedly, the refusal to acknowledge the awful harm done

to blacks by slavery is a willful ignorance that smacks of arrogance. It is like the majority saying, "Who cares about the minority? Who needs Negroes?" There is some value in contemporary white America knowing the facts about slavery practiced in the land of the free and the home of the brave. As someone has said, whites benefit from "affirmative acceptance."

No man is an island, not even the black American. *All* Americans have benefited by the labors of others, whether those who preceded them were slave or free, black or white. All is not "peaches and cream" for the white man. His sinful heart has taken *advantage* of the so-called *advantages*. The result: suicide, homosexuality, abortion, fraud, gross immorality, treason, mass murder, church bombings, hypocrisy, and racial arrogance. Is he happy with his *advantages*? I think not.

All is not "rotten peaches and sour cream" for the black man. We are living longer, the literacy rate is up, political doors have opened, unemployment rate has decreased, the church still holds a prominent place in black society (though decreasing in influence), and overall, compared with third world countries, we are better off. Is he happy with his lot? I think not, judging from the desire for reparation, the bitterness that is a byproduct of ingratitude to God, and the many acts of self-destructiveness in black society.

Dr. Ron Sider speaks much about corporate guilt and institutional evil. His argument is Old Testamenty (that's not quite the same as Old Testamental). There is the failure to realize that under a Theocratic government (which no longer exists as such), the Jews trained in religion were in a covenant relationship with God, as no other people in the history of mankind. All humans suffer because of sin, whether they are Christians or not. I am afflicted by the sins of others, but this is not to say a part of me is sinning when another man, believer or unbeliever, sins.

There is no New Testament Church Letter basis for

contemporary Christians to confess the sins of their ancestors. God does not hold me accountable for the evils perpetrated by those who preceded me. My teeth are not set on edge because my forefathers ate sour grapes. In no way am I held responsible by God for the evils committed by earlier generations. I rejoice in that the wickedness which men have done, even the evil of black slavery, has been turned into good by the God of the Bible (Genesis 50.20).

GOD MAKES GOOD COME OUT OF EVIL

Regardless of the hypocrisy of some who sought to approve slavery by rationalizing that the slave trade civilized the Africans, or that it gave the savages an opportunity to become Christians, the fact is, these two things actually took place. Some Africanists resent being told this. They claim the Africans had their own religion. This is true, they did, but it was idolatrous. They did not serve the one and only true God, the God of the Bible, the Father of our Lord and Savior, Jesus Christ.

Note the boldness of the apostle Paul at Corinth and at Ephesus. The saints at Corinth were told *"that the things which the Gentiles sacrifice they sacrifice to demons and not to God..."* (1 Corinthians 10.20). Prior to becoming Christians, the believers at Ephesus were told, *"that at that time you were without Christ, being aliens from the commonwealth of Israel and strangers from the covenants of promise, **having no hope and without God in the world...**"* (Ephesians 2.12).

Why should we not teach that even blacks (as well as whites) without Christ are lost!

The Christian church is the body of Jesus Christ. Whatever happens to one member of the body effects the entire body (1

Corinthians 12.26). We believers deal with the present tense, for we do have an obligation to treat all people fairly. However, what we call "institutional evil," and "structural injustice" are matters which we Christians have no power to eliminate. Our calling is to spread the Gospel of the shed blood of Jesus Christ as the only way to eternal salvation. Of course, we speak out against all forms of evil, for that is our mandate.

This approach is considered "far too individualistic, an atomistic view of sin and guilt." However, we are not convinced that it is biblical for members of the Church Age to "confess the sins of one's fathers and contemporaries." Isaiah confessed that he was a sinner precisely because of Israel's rebellion and disobedience against the God who had established a covenant relationship with them, and Who in grace called them "His people."

According to the Bible we live in a world-system (*kosmos*) ruled by the Devil, the prince of this world-age (*aion*). Realism moves us to accept Paul's statement that to avoid immorality we "would need to go out of the world" (1 Corinthians 5.10). The racist sins against me, a black man.

Nevertheless, I do not share his sinning, for this would be self-destructive. My suffering is moral unless I retaliate in resentment and hatred, in which case I sin and put myself on his low level.

Understand then that all of this is on a personal, one-to-one relationship, not some concept of a corporate operation. Christ did not establish an Abolitionist Society to get rid of slavery in His day, with a Malcolm X "by any means necessary" thrust. He did not organize a secret army to overthrow the Roman Government.

The apostle Paul started no political party or rebellion against what is called "institutionalized evil." In the very midst of persecution, Simon Peter exhorted the saints to practice godliness whereby they could put to silence those who would falsely accuse them.

IS GUILT INHERITED?

Our interpretation of the Bible moves us to reject holding contemporary Americans responsible for the effects of slavery. Robinson disagrees (230), and calls my stance the habit of America rubbing "itself with the memory-emptying salve of contemporaneousness." He speaks of contemporary America shouldering responsibility for those wrongs committed "by a younger America ... until such wrongs have been adequately compensated and righted." *How* can we pay for such wrongs and make restitution?

We concur with Thomas Sowell (219) that "the heritability of guilt is a principle without foundation and dangerously divisive in any society ... No society could survive historical compensation as a general principle. Doing justice among contemporaries is more than enough challenge." Sowell stated that acceptance of the heritability of guilt as a principle would mean that the present generation of Jews "would be justified in putting this generation of Germans in concentration camps." We agree with him that no sane adult believes this.

As far as numbers are concerned, the reparationist is forced to emphasize what is happening racially in America today, rather than what occurred in slavery of yesteryear. The reason for this is that the majority of white Americans do not have roots deep enough to link them with the institution of slavery in the U.S. There is the suggestion then that in proportion to the percentage of the population, more blacks have deeper roots in America than whites do. Add to this the numbers of white families that never owned slaves prior to 1865. Missing slave receipts make it difficult if not impossible for many whites to report accurately their family tree.

Some whites feel a sense of complicity in the oppressive black slavery practiced by those who preceded them. How does one know that this concern, this sense of guilt is legitimate, and heartfelt, and not the product of having been manipulated or victimized by rhetoric? Are there really two camps, or just one--victims?

Who makes the distinction? Is it correct to say that the white man who has profited in some way or degree by slave labor inherited that profitability, and therefore he should make restitution? All gains are based upon the labors of others. The apostle asks, "What do you have that was not given to you?" (1 Corinthians 4.7). Think this question through, and see if it affects your interpretation of heritability and what is called the "debt of the past."

Black reparation is a policy that victimizes innocent whites. "The question of what responsibility 'whites' have for what 'whites' did in this country is one fraught with complexities and contradictions. Even white Southerners who are the direct descendants of people who several generations ago were slave owners may feel it is unjustified to hold them responsible for acts committed before they were born" (Wachtel, 252).

One white man said, "By the way, as a descendant of Anglo-

Saxons, I've been deeply traumatized by what the Normans did to us in 1066. How about some reparations for me too?" You see then the complexities, contradictions and problems dealing with the matter of responsibility for the evils of slavery past and for present lingering results of previous servitude.

We wish we could set right the "inhumanity, brutality, and viciousness" of slavery. "But there are no more futile or dangerous efforts than attempts to redress the wrongs of history ... The biological or cultural continuity of a people does not make guilt inheritable ... Nor can the particular economic and social consequences of particular past actions necessarily be isolated or quantified in the lives of contemporaries --- not when innumerable other influences have intervened in the meantime" (Sowell, 251).

Summary: We hear the voices of whites protesting any idea of inherited culpability concerning black slavery or its aftermath. But more than these vocal and written protests is the moral issue. We are convinced that from a biblical point of view, the concept of one generation being held accountable or liable for the evils of a preceding generation is immoral.

What we have inherited is the sin nature. When Adam sinned, we sinned, so declares the Sovereign God of the Bible (Romans 5). From the sin nature issue all kinds of sins, and each human being is held responsible for these personal sins. Each tub stands on its own bottom. There is no "passing the buck" here. Neither Adam's protest, "The woman whom You gave to be with me, she gave me of the tree, and I ate," nor Eve's protest, "The serpent deceived me, and I ate," is acceptable by God (Genesis 3.12-13).

Universal sin allows no fingerpointing at the individual sins of any one generation or group of people; it permits no passing down to their descendants any responsibility for making restitution for the results of those transgressions. Contemporaries have enough trouble dealing with their own wickedness and the present-day wages of sin.

You can see why Jehovah forbade the Israelites to use the proverb, "The fathers have eaten sour grapes, and the children's teeth are set on edge" (Ezekiel 18.2-3; Jeremiah 31.29-30). The warning comes to black Americans: Beware, lest seeking reparation and blaming others for *their* sins, "inherited" and otherwise, we fail to see *our own* willfully sinful behavior. And fail to recognize that insistence on being paid reparation because we are descendants of American slaves is in itself an immoral demand!

CONCLUSIONS

I do not desire to play down the horror of slavery, or its many evil aftereffects. Slavery -- its cruelty, brutality, disregard for human dignity, rape and murder -- ever remains a splotch on the character of America.

Let no one say that I favor racism because I disapprove of black reparation . The God of the Bible is no respecter of persons, no receiver of faces or races; and in His presence no flesh shall glory!

In summary then, here are my thoughts and reasons why the descendants of black slaves should not receive a penny in reparation; and why the movement will be a total failure.

1. Paying reparation would accomplish no permanent good. The money would not last, eliminate racism, and blacks would not be satisfied. Even as the payment of "forty acres and a mule" would not have solved the problems created by slavery, so no amount of money will ameliorate slavery's aftermath.

2. There will never be agreement on the amount of money needed for reparation, or agreement on how to spend the money.

3. The demand for reparation stirs up feelings of guilt, without creating at the same time heart repentance. Furthermore, the charges that Jews, the Christian church, and missionaries are responsible for black slavery are baseless.

4. White paternalism would remain. Perhaps feeling forced to make reparation payment, the paternalist would seek other avenues to perpetuate his feelings of superiority.

5. Blacks are not in slavery now. We are American citizens, and efforts to put present-day racism on the same level with slavery are foolish.

6. Reparationists appear to be aware that money can never pay for the broken families, heartbreak, suffering, and indignity suffered by blacks in America. However, it has been difficult for

me to get rid of the feeling that their insistence upon reparation somehow masks or disguises a hope and desire to experience satisfaction by a reparation payment for such suffering.

7. The Bible accounts of the Exodus (the Jews leaving Egypt), of Zacchaeus repaying those he had cheated, and of James' demand that laborers be paid, teach the concept of reparation. However, the dissimilarities -- in circumstances, motives, and spirituality -- between these Bible accounts and black reparation make it inappropriate to use them for support of black reparation.

8. Failure to indict Africans who sold Africans into slavery smacks of racism on the part of the reparation movement. Failure to give Islam its shameful share of credit in the slave trade may also point to those blacks who embrace Islam while claiming that Christianity is "the white man's religion."

9. Inasmuch as all blacks who were slaves in the U.S. are dead, the weight falls on reparationists to determine who the direct descendants of the American slaves are. This is a formidable, yea, impossible task.

10. The problems associated with deciding who pays and who receives remuneration are hugely complex, and unsolvable. Here is why: (a) Africans sold Africans into slavery (b) Europeans sold Africans into slavery (c) Arabs sold Africans into slavery (d) Native Americans owned slaves (e) Blacks in America owned slaves. Obviously, it is not fair to select the descendants of the white Europeans as the culprits, while ignoring the culpability of the other groups. Besides, who and where are the descendants of these people who were active in the slave trade and ownership?

11. There ever remains the question of the morality of holding contemporary white Americans -- regardless of how deep their roots may go -- responsible for the sins of their ancestors or the sins of all early (colonial) white Americans!

12. Entirely too much weight is put upon human efforts to overcome spiritual problems. Indeed, secular humanism is at the very heart of the reparation movement. Neither laws nor money

can solve the sin problem inherent in the heart of mankind.

13. I fear that many reparationists are not aware of the bitterness in their hearts, a bitterness perhaps born of the desire for revenge, or even hatred of whites -- a bitterness that has blinded them to the futility of the goal they seek. Reparation is not the road to follow. It is a movement that fails to express gratitude to God for even living in America, and enjoying the many freedoms we do have.

14. Can it be determined actually that slavery benefited America? If it has not benefited the country, what is there to share with the descendants of slaves? Is it possible to assign a dollar value to the lives lost in the Civil War, and to the results of immorality, race hatred, the disruption of family life, lost gifts and talents -- is it possible to assign a dollar value to these evils, and then subtract that amount from the value of the physical work done by the slaves?

15. Blacks have made great achievements in America. The drive to persevere and overcome must continue. We must not allow the reparation movement to make meaningless the words, "We shall overcome!" Christians are especially mindful that without Jesus Christ we cannot accomplish anything of permanent value; but through Christ, Who strengthens us, we can do all things!

APPENDIX A - THE BLACK MANIFESTO

I. The Black Manifesto Introduction

We have come from all over the country, burning with anger and despair not only with the miserable economic plight of our people, but fully aware that the racism on which the Western World was built dominates our lives. There can be no separation of the problems of racism from the problems of our economic, political, and cultural degradation. To any black man, this is clear. But there are still some of our people who are clinging to the rhetoric of the Negro and we must separate ourselves from those Negroes who go around the country promoting all types of schemes for Black Capitalism.

Ironically, some of the most militant Black Nationalists, as they call themselves, have been the first to jump on the bandwagon of black capitalism. They are pimps, Black Power Pimps and fraudulent leaders and the people must be educated to understand that any black man or Negro who is advocating a perpetuation of capitalism inside the United States is in fact seeking not only his ultimate destruction and death, but is contributing to the exploitation of black people all around the world. For it is the power of the United States Government, this racist, imperialist government that is choking the life of all people around the world.

We are an African people. We sit back and watch the Jews in this country make Israel a powerful conservative state in the Middle East, but we are not concerned actively about the plight of our brothers in Africa. We are the most advanced technological group of black people in the world, and there are many skills that could be offered to Africa. At the same time, it must be publicly stated that many African leaders are in disarray themselves, having been duped into following the lines as laid out by the Western Imperialist governments.

Africans themselves succumbed to and are victims of the power of the United States. For instance, during the summer of 1967, as the representatives of SNCC, Howard Moore and I traveled extensively in Tanzania and Zambia. We talked to high, very high, government officials. We told them there were many black people in the United States who were willing to come and work in Africa. All these government officials, who were part of the leadership in their respective governments, said they wanted us to send as many skilled people that we could contact. But this program never came into fruition and we do not know the exact reasons, for I assure you that we talked and were committed to making this a successful program. It is our guess that the United States put the squeeze on these countries, for such a program directed by SNCC would have been too dangerous to the international prestige of the U.S. It is also possible that some of the wild statements by some black leader frightened the Africans.

In Africa today, there is great suspicion of black people in this country. This is a correct suspicion since most of the Negroes who have left the States for work in Africa usually work for the Central Intelligence Agency (CIA) or the State Department. But the respect for us as a people continues to mount and the day will come when we can return to our homeland as brothers and sisters. But we should not think of going back to Africa today, for we are located in a Strategic position. We live inside the U.S. which is the *most barbaric country in the world* and we have a chance to *help bring this government down*.

Time is short and we do not have much time and it is time we stop mincing words. Caution is fine, but no oppressed people ever gained their Liberation until they were ready to fight, to use whatever means necessary, including the use of force and power of the gun to bring down the colonizer.

We have heard the rhetoric, but we have not heard the rhetoric which says that black people in this country must understand that we are the Vanguard Force. We shall liberate all people in the U.S. and we will be instrumental in the liberation of colored people the world around. We must understand this point very clearly so that we are not trapped into diversionary and reactionary movements.

Any class analysis of the U.S. shows very clearly that black people are the most oppressed group of people inside the United States. We have suffered the most from racism and exploitation, cultural degradation and lack of political power. It follows from the laws of revolution that the most oppressed will make the revolution, but we are not talking about just making the revolution. All the parties on the left who consider themselves revolutionary will say that blacks are the Vanguard, but we must assume leadership, total control and we must exercise the humanity which is inherent in us. We are the most humane people within the U.S. We have suffered and we understand suffering. Our hearts go out to the Vietnamese for we know what it is to suffer under the domination of racist America. Our hearts, our soul and all the compassion we can mount goes out to our brothers in Africa, Santa Domingo, Latin America and Asia who are being tricked by the power structure of the U.S. which is dominating the world today.

These ruthless, barbaric men have systematically tried to kill all people and organizations opposed to its imperialism. We no longer can just get by with the use of the word capitalism to describe the U.S., for it is an imperial power, sending money, *missionaries* and the army throughout the world to protect this government and the few rich whites who control it. General Motors and all the major auto industries are operating in South Africa, yet the white-dominated leadership of the United Auto Workers sees no relationship to the exploitation of black people in South Africa and the exploitation of black people in the U.S. If they understand it, they certainly do not put it into practice which is the actual test. We as black people must be concerned with the total conditions of all black people in the world.

But while we talk of revolution which will be an armed confrontation and long years of sustained guerrilla warfare inside this country, we must also talk of the type of world we want to live in. We must commit ourselves to a society where the total means of production are taken from the rich and placed into the hands of the state for the welfare of all the people. This is what we mean when we say total control. And we mean that black people who have suffered the most from exploitation and racism must move to protect their black interests by assuming leadership inside of the United States of everything that exists. The time has passed when we are second in command and the white boy stands on top. This is especially true of the Welfare Agencies in this country, but it is not enough to say that a black man is on top. He must be committed to building the new society, to taking the wealth away from the rich people such as General Motors, Ford, Chrysler, the Du Points, the Rockefeller, the Melons, and all the other rich white exploiters and racists who run this world.

Where do we begin? We have already started. We started the moment we were brought to this country. In fact, we started on the shores of Africa, for we have always resisted attempts to make us slaves and now we must resist the attempts to make us capitalists, for this will be the same line as that of integration into the mainstream of American life. Therefore, brothers and sisters, there is no need to fall into the trap that we have to get an ideology. We HAVE an ideology. Our fight is against racism, capitalism and imperialism and we are dedicated to building a socialist society inside the United States where the total means of production and distribution are in the hands of the State and that must be led by black people, by revolutionary blacks who are concerned about the total humanity of this world. And, therefore, we obviously are different from some of those who seek a black nation in the United States, for there is no way for that nation to be viable if in fact the United States remains in the hands of white racists. Then too, let us deal with some arguments that we should share power with whites. We say that there must be a revolutionary black Vanguard and that white people in this country must be willing to accept black leadership, for that is the only protection that black people have to protect ourselves from racism rising again in this country.

Racism in the U.S. is so pervasive in the mentality of whites that only an armed, well-disciplined, black-controlled government can insure the stamping out of racism in this country. And that is why we plead with black people not to be talking about a few crumbs, a few thousand dollars for this cooperative, or a thousand dollars which splits black people into fighting over the dollar. That is the intention of the government. We say ... think in terms of total control of the U.S. Prepare ourselves to *seize state power*. Do not hedge, for time is short and all around the world the forces of liberation are directing their attacks against the U.S. It is a powerful country, but that power is not greater than that of black people. We work the chief industries in this country and we could cripple the economy while the brothers fought guerrilla warfare in the streets. This will take some long range planning, but whether it happens in a thousand years is of no consequence. It cannot happen unless we start. How then is all of this related to this conference?

First of all, this conference is called by a set of religious people, Christians, who have been involved in the exploitation and rape of black people since the country was founded. The missionary goes hand in hand with the power of the states. We must begin seizing power wherever we are and we must say to the planners of this conference that you are no longer in charge. We the people who have assembled here thank you for getting us here, but we are going to assume power over the conference and determine from this moment on the direction in which we want to go. We are not saying that the conference was planned badly. The staff of the conference has worked hard and have done a magnificent job in bringing all of us together and we must include them in the new membership which must surface from this point on. The conference is now the property of the people who are assembled here. This we proclaim as fact and not rhetoric and there are demands that we are going to make and we insist that they help implement.

We maintain we have the revolutionary right to do this. We

have the same rights, if you will, as the *Christians* had in going into Africa and raping our Motherland and bringing us away from our continent of peace and into this hostile and alien environment where we have been living in perpetual warfare since 1619. Our seizure of power at this conference is based on a program and our program is contained in the MANIFESTO.

II. Black Manifesto

We the black people assembled in Detroit, Michigan for the National Black Economic Development Conference are fully aware that we have been forced to come together because *racist white America has exploited* our resources, our minds, our bodies, our labor. For centuries we have been forced to live as colonized people inside the United States, victimized by the most vicious, racist system in the world. We have helped to build the most industrial country in the world.

We are *therefore* demanding of the white Christian *churches* and Jewish synagogues which are part and parcel of the system of capitalism, that they begin to pay reparations to black people in this country. We are demanding $500,000,000 from the Christian white churches and the Jewish synagogues. This total comes to *15 dollars per nigger*. This is a low estimate for we maintain there are probably more than 30,000,000 black people in this country. $15 a nigger is not a large sum of money and we know that the churches and synagogues have a tremendous wealth and its membership, white America, has profited and still exploits black people. We are also not unaware that the exploitation of colored peoples around the world is aided and abetted by the white Christian churches and synagogues. This demand for $500,000,000 is not an idle resolution or empty words. Fifteen dollars for every black brother and sister in the United States is only *a beginning* of the reparations due us as people who have been exploited and degraded, brutalized, killed and persecuted. Underneath all of this exploitation, the racism of this country had produced a psychological effect upon us that we are beginning to shake off. We are no longer afraid to demand our full rights as a people in this decadent society.

We are demanding $500,000,000 to be spent in the following way:

1. We call for the establishment of a Southern land bank to help our brothers and sisters who have to leave their land because of racist pressure for people who want to establish cooperative farms, but who have no funds. We have seen too many farmers evicted from their homes because they have dared to defy the white racism of this country. We need money for land. We must fight for massive sums of money for this Southern Land Bank. We call for $200,000,000 to implement this program.

2. We call for the establishment of four major publishing and printing industries in the United States to be funded with ten million dollars each. These publishing houses are to be located in Detroit, Atlanta, Los Angeles, and New York. They will help to generate capital for further cooperative investments in the black community, provide jobs and an alternative to the white-dominated and controlled printing field.

3. We call for the establishment of four of the most advanced scientific and futuristic audio-visual networks to be located in Detroit, Chicago, Cleveland and Washington, D.C. These TV networks will provide an alternative to the racist propaganda that fills the current television networks. Each of these TV networks will be funded by ten million dollars each.

4. We call for a research skills center which will provide research on the problems of black people. This center must be funded with no less than 30 million dollars.

5. We call for the establishment of a training center for the teaching of skills in community organization, photography, movie

making, television making and repair, radio building and repair and all other skills needed in communication. This training center shall be funded with no less than ten million dollars.

    6. We recognize the role of the National Welfare Rights Organization and we intend to work with them. We call for ten million dollars to assist in the organization of welfare recipients. We want to organize the welfare workers in this country so that they may demand more money from the government and better administration of the welfare system of this country.

    7. We call for $20,000,000 to establish a National Black Labor Strike and Defense Fund. This is necessary for the protection of black workers and their families who are fighting racist working conditions in this country.

    *8. We call for the establishment of the International Black Appeal (IBA). This International Black Appeal will be funded with no less than $20,000,000. The IBA is charged with producing more capital for the establishment of cooperative businesses in the United States and Africa, our Motherland. The International Black Appeal is one of the most important demands that we are making for we know that it can generate and raise funds throughout the United States and help our African brothers. The IBA is charged with three functions and shall be headed by James Forman:

    (a) Raising money for the program of the National Black Economic Development Conference.

    (b) The development of cooperatives in African countries and support of African Liberation movements.

    (c) Establishment of a Black Anti-Defamation League which will protect our African image.

*Revised and approved by Steering Committee

    9. We call for the establishment of a Black University to be funded with $130,000,000 to be located in the South. Negotiations are presently under way with a Southern University.

10. We demand that IFCO allocate all unused funds in the planning budget to implement the demands of this conference.

In order to win our demands we are aware that we will have to have massive support, therefore:

(1) We call upon all black people throughout the United States to consider themselves as members of the National Black Economic Development Conference and to act in unity to help force the racist white Christian churches and Jewish synagogues to implement these demands.

(2) We call upon all the concerned black people across the country to contact black workers, black women, black students and the black unemployed, community groups, welfare organizations, teacher organizations, church leaders and organizations explaining how these demands are vital to the black community of the U.S. Pressure by whatever means necessary should be applied to the white power structure of the racist white Christian churches and Jewish synagogues. All black people should act boldly in confronting our white oppressors and demanding this modest reparation of 15 dollars per black man.

(3) Delegates and members of the National Black Economic Development Conference are urged to call press conferences in the cities and to attempt to get as many black organizations as possible to support the demands of the conference. The quick use of the press in the local areas will heighten the tension and these demands must be attempted to be won in a short period of time, although we are prepared for protracted and long range struggle.

(4) We call for the total disruption of selected church sponsored agencies operating anywhere in the U.S. and the world. Black workers, black women, black students and the black unemployed are encouraged to seize the offices, telephones, and printing apparatus of all church sponsored agencies and to hold these in trusteeship until our demands are met.

(5) We call upon all delegates and members of the National Black Economic Development Conference to stage sit-in demonstrations at selected black and white churches. This is not to be interpreted as a continuation of the sit-in movement of the early sixties but we know that active confrontation inside white churches is possible and will strengthen the possibility of meeting our demands. Such confrontation can take the form of reading the Black Manifesto instead of a sermon or passing it out to church members. The principle of self-defense should be applied if attacked.

(6) On May 4, 1969, or a date thereafter, depending upon local conditions, we call upon black people to commence the disruption of the racist churches and synagogues throughout the United States.

(7) We call upon IFCO to serve as a central staff to coordinate the mandate of the conference and to reproduce and distribute en mass literature, leaflets, news items, press releases and other material.

(8) We call upon all delegates to find within the white community those forces which will work under the leadership of blacks to implement these demands by whatever means necessary. By taking such actions, white Americans will demonstrate concretely that they are willing to fight the white skin privilege and the white supremacy and racism which has forced us as black people to make these demands.

(9) We call upon all white Christians and Jews to practice patience, tolerance, understanding and nonviolence as they have encouraged, advised and demanded that we as black people should do throughout our entire enforced slavery in the United States. The true test of their faith and belief in the Cross and the words of the prophets will certainly be put to test as we seek legitimate and extremely modest reparations for our role in developing the industrial base of the Western World through our slave labor. But

we are no longer slaves, we are men and women, proud of our African heritage, determined to have our dignity.

(10) We are so proud of our African heritage and realize concretely that our struggle is not only to make revolution in the United States, but to protect our brothers and sisters in Africa and to help them rid themselves of racism, capitalism, and imperialism by whatever means necessary, including armed struggle. We are and must be willing to fight the defamation of our African image wherever it rears its ugly head. We are therefore charging the Steering Committee to create a Black Anti-Defamation League to be funded by money raised from the International Black Appeal.

(11) We fully recognize that revolution in the United States and Africa, our Motherland, is more than a one dimensional operation. It will require the total integration of the political, economic, and military components and therefore, we call upon all our brothers and sisters who have acquired training and expertise in the fields of engineering, electronics, research, community organization, physics, biology, chemistry, mathematics, medicine, military science and warfare to assist the National Black Economic Development Conference in the implementation of its program.

(12) To implement these demands we must have a fearless leadership. We must have a leadership which is willing to battle the church establishment to implement these demands. To win our demands we will have to declare war on the white Christian churches and synagogues and this means we may have to fight the total government structure of this country. Let no one here think that these demands will be met by our mere stating them. For the sake of the churches and synagogues, we hope that they have the wisdom to understand that these demands are modest and reasonable. But if the white Christians and Jews are not willing to meet our demands through peace and good will, then we declare war and are prepared to fight by whatever means necessary. We are, therefore, proposing the election of the following Steering

Committee:
- Lucious Walker
- Renny Freeman
- Luke Tripp
- Howard Fuller
- James Forman
- John Watson
- Dan Aldridge
- John Williams
- Ken Cockrel
- Chuck Wooten
- Fannie Lou Hamer
- Julian Bond
- Mark Comfort
- Earl Allen
- Robert Browne
- Vincent Harding
- Mike Hamlin
- Len Holt
- Peter Bernard
- Michael Wright
- Muhammed Kenyatta
- Mel Jackson
- Howard Moore
- Harold Holmes

Brothers and sisters, we no longer are shuffling our feet and scratching our heads. We are tall, black and proud. And we say to the white Christian churches and Jewish synagogues, to the government of this country and to all the white racist imperialists who compose it, there is only one thing left that you can do to further degrade black people and that is to kill us. But we have been dying too long for this country. We have died in every war. We are dying in Vietnam today fighting the wrong enemy.

The new black man wants to live and to live means that we must not become static or merely believe in self-defense. We must boldly go out and attack the white Western world at its power centers. The white Christian churches are another form of government in this country and they are used by the government of this country to exploit the people of Latin America, Asia and Africa, but the day is soon coming to an end. Therefore, brothers and sisters, the demands we make upon the white Christian churches and the Jewish synagogues are small demands. They represent 15 dollars per black person in these United States. We can legitimately demand this from the church power structure. We must demand more from the United States Government.

But to win our demands from the church which is linked up with the United States Government, we must not forget that it will ultimately be by force and power that we will win.

We are not threatening the churches. We are saying that we know the churches came with the military might of the colonizers and have been sustained by the military might of the colonizers. Hence, if the churches in colonial territories were established by military might, we know deep within our hearts that we must be prepared to use force to get our demands. We are not saying that this is the road we want to take. It is not, but let us be very clear that we are not opposed to force and we are not opposed to violence. We were captured in Africa by violence. We were kept in bondage and political servitude and forced to work as slaves by the military machinery and the Christian church working hand in hand.

We recognize that in issuing this manifesto we must prepare for a long range educational campaign in all communities of this country, but we know that the Christian churches have contributed to our oppression in white America. We do not intend to abuse our black brothers and sisters in black churches who have uncritically accepted Christianity. We want them to understand how the racist white Christian church with its hypocritical declarations and doctrines of brotherhood has abused our trust and faith. An attack on the religious beliefs of black people is not our major objective, even though we know that we were not Christians when we were brought to this country, but that Christianity was used to help enslave us. Our objective in issuing this Manifesto is to force the racist white Christian church to begin the payment of reparations which are due to all black people, not only by the Church but also by private business and the U.S. government. We see this focus on the Christian church as an effort around which all black people can unite.

Our demands are negotiable, but they cannot be minimized,

they can only be increased and the Church is asked to come up with larger sums of money than we are asking. Our slogans are:

ALL ROADS MUST LEAD TO REVOLUTION
UNITE WITH WHOMEVER YOU CAN UNITE
NEUTRALIZE WHEREVER POSSIBLE
FIGHT OUR ENEMIES RELENTLESSLY
VICTORY TO THE PEOPLE
LIFE AND GOOD HEALTH TO MANKIND
RESISTANCE TO DOMINATION BY THE WHITE CHRISTIAN CHURCHES AND THE JEWISH SYNAGOGUES
REVOLUTIONARY BLACK POWER
WE SHALL WIN WITHOUT A DOUBT

APPENDIX B - TEN REASONS WHY REPARATIONS FOR BLACKS IS A BAD IDEA *FOR BLACKS* AND RACIST TOO
- David Horowitz, Editor-in-Chief, *FrontpageMagazine. com,* 3 Jan 01, president *Center for the Study of Popular Culture.*

1. There is No Single Group Clearly Responsible for the Crime of Slavery: Black Africans and Arabs were responsible for enslaving the ancestors of African-Americans. There were 3,000 black slave-owners in the ante-bellum United States. Are reparations to be paid by *their* descendants too?

2. There is No One Group that Benefited Exclusively from Its Fruits: The claim for reparations is premised on the false assumption that only whites have benefited from slavery. If slave labor created wealth for Americans, then obviously it has created wealth for black Americans as well, including the descendants of slaves.

The GNP of black America is so large that it makes the African-American community the 10th most prosperous "nation" in the world. American blacks *on average* enjoy per capita incomes in the range of twenty to *fifty* times that of blacks living in any of the African nations from which they were kidnapped.

3. Only a Tiny Minority of White Americans Ever Owned Slaves, and Others Gave Their Lives to Free Them: Only a tiny minority of Americans ever owned slaves. This is true even for those who lived in the ante-bellum South where only one white in five was a slaveholder. Why should *their* descendants owe a debt? What about the descendants of the 350,000 Union soldiers who died to free the slaves? They gave their lives. What possible moral principle would ask them to pay (through their descendants) again?

4. America Today Is a Multi-Ethnic Nation and Most Americans Have No Connection (Direct or Indirect) to Slavery: The two great waves of American immigration occurred after 1880 and then after 1960. What rationale would require Vietnamese boat people, Russian refuseniks, Iranian refugees, and Armenian victims of the Turkish persecution, Jews, Mexicans, Greeks, or Polish, Hungarian, Cambodian and Korean victims of Communism, to pay reparations to American blacks?

5. The Historical Precedents Used to Justify the Reparations Claim Do Not Apply, and the Claim Itself Is Based on Race Not Injury: The historical precedents generally invoked to justify the reparations claim are payments to Jewish survivors of the Holocaust, Japanese-Americans and African-American victims of racial experiments in Tuskegee, or racial outrages in Rosewood and Oklahoma City. But in each case, the recipients of reparations were the direct victims of the injustice or their immediate families. This would be the only case of reparations to people who were not immediately affected and whose sole qualification to receive reparations would be racial.

As has already been pointed out, during the slavery era, many blacks were free men or slave-owners themselves, yet the reparations claimants make no distinction between the roles blacks actually played in the injustice itself. Randall Robinson's book on reparations, *The Debt*, which is the manifesto of the reparations movement is politically sub-titled, "What America Owes to Blacks." If this is not racism, what is?

6. The Reparations Argument Is Based on the Unfounded Claim that All African-American Descendants of Slaves Suffer from the Economic Consequences of Slavery and Discrimination: No evidence-based attempt has been made to prove that living individuals have been adversely affected by a slave system that was ended over 150 years ago. But there is plenty of evidence that hardships that occurred were hardships that individuals could and did overcome. The black middle-class in America is a prosperous community that is now larger in absolute terms than the black underclass. Does its existence not suggest that economic adversity is the result of failures of individual character rather than the lingering after-effects of racial discrimination and a slave system that ceased to exist well over a century ago? West Indian blacks in America are also descended from slaves but their average incomes are equiva-lent to the average incomes of whites (and nearly 25% higher than the average incomes of American born blacks). How is it that slavery adversely affected one large group of descendants but not the other? How can government be expected to decide an issue that is so subjective -- and yet so critical -- to the case?

7. The Reparations Claim Is One More Attempt to Turn African-Americans into Victims. It Sends a Damaging Message to the African-American Community: The renewed sense of grievance -- which is what the claim for reparations will inevitably create -- is neither a constructive nor a helpful message for black leaders to be sending to their communities and to others. To focus the social passions of African-Americans on what some Americans may have done to their ancestors fifty or a hundred and fifty years ago is to burden them with a crippling sense of victim-hood. How are the millions of refugees from tyranny and genocide who are now living in American going to receive these claims, moreover, except as demands for special treatment, an extravagant new handout that is only necessary because some blacks can't seem to locate the ladder of opportunity within reach of others -- many less privileged than themselves?

8. Reparations to African Americans Have Already Been Paid: Since the passage of the Civil Rights Acts and the advent of the Great Society in 1965, trillions of dollars in transfer payments have been made to African-Americans in the form of welfare benefits and racial preferences (in contracts, job placements and educational admissions) -- all under the rationale of redressing historical racial grievances. It is said that reparations are necessary to achieve a healing between African-Americans and other Americans. If trillion dollar restitutions and a wholesale rewriting of American law (in order to accommodate racial preferences) for African-Americans is not enough to achieve a "healing," what *will*?

9. What About the Debt Blacks Owe to America?: Slavery existed for thousands of years before the Atlantic slave trade was born, and in all societies. But in the thousand years of its existence, there never was an anti-slavery movement until white Christians --Englishmen and Americans -- created one. If not for the anti-slavery attitudes and military power of white Englishmen and Americans, the slave trade would not have been brought to an end. If not for the sacrifices of white soldiers and a white American president who gave his life to sign the Emancipation Proclamation, blacks in America would *still* be slaves.

If not for the dedication of Americans of all ethnicities and colors to a society based on the principle that all men are created equal, blacks in America would not enjoy the highest standard of living of blacks anywhere in the world, and indeed one of the highest standards of living of any people in the world. They would not enjoy the greatest freedoms and the most thoroughly protected individual rights anywhere. Where is the gratitude of black America and its leaders for those *gifts*?

10. The Reparations Claim Is a Separatist Idea that Sets African-Americans Against the Nation that Gave Them Freedom: Blacks were here before the Mayflower. Who is more American than the descendants of African slaves? For the African-American community to isolate itself even further from America is to embark on a course whose implications are troubling. Yet the African-American community has had a long-running flirtation with separatists, nationalists and the political left, who want African-Americans to be no part of America's social contract. African Americans should reject this temptation. For all America's faults, African-Americans have an enormous stake in their country and its heritage. It is this heritage that is really under attack by the reparations movement. The reparations claim is one more assault on America, conducted by racial separatists and the political left. It is an attack not only on white Americans, but on all Americans -- especially African-Americans. America's African-American citizens are the richest and most privileged black people alive -- a bounty that is a direct result of the heritage that is under assault. The American ideal needs the support of its African-American citizens. But African-Americans also need the support of the American idea. For it is this idea that led to the principles and institutions that have set African-Americans -- and all of us -- free.

ENDNOTES

Chapter 1 - Background and Definitions

1. The census of 1860 showed that the eleven Confederate states had a population of 5,449,467 whites and 3,521,111 slaves" (Paul Johnson, *A History of the American People*, 462).

Chapter 2 - Renewed Interest

1. Obituary, *The Philadelphia Inquirer*, 7 Jan 1992.
2. Conyer's inflated rhetoric is not likely to win him supporters, states Barkan: 292. The congressman is reported as saying, "African Americans are still victims of slavery as surely as those who lived under its confinement."
3. For more information, see chapter 4, The Jews, the Holocaust and Black Slavery.
4. Munford, 415: "Although American Indians continue to be shortchanged in all emoluments that make human existence tolerable, the federal government has at least sporadically recognized the principle of reparations in respect to aboriginals, distributing one billion dollars and 44 million acres of land to the Native Americans of Alaska; $23 million (N'COBRA says, $32 million) to the Ottawas of Michigan (1986); $81 million to the Klamaths of Oregon (1980); $31 million to the Chippewas of Wisconsin; $12.3 million to the Florida descendants of the Seminole holocaust (1985); and $105 million to the Sioux of "South Dakota (1985)."
5. Cf. Barkan, "A Massacre at Rosewood," 296-299.
6. Cf. "Ten Reasons Why Considering Reparations is a Good Idea for Americans, and Horowitz too," by Earl Ofari Hutchinson, President of The National Alliance for Positive Action<

http:/www. natalliance.org>, 30 Mar 2001. See also Horowitz's reply: FrontPagemag.com 5 Jun 2000.

7. Prompt conscription of blacks "would have enormously added to the strength of the Confederate armies. And most of them [slaves] would have been willing to fight for the South, too--after all, it was their way of life as well as that of the whites which was at stake. It is a curious paradox, but one typical of the ironies of history, that black participation might conceivably have turned the scales in the South's favor. But obstinacy and 'theory' won the day and few blacks actually got the chance to fight for their homeland" (Johnson, 493). I wonder what the black reparationists think of this statement?

8. President Lincoln realized "that if he did preserve the Union, slavery would go anyway." He replied to Horace Greely, who had accused him of failing to emancipate the slaves: "My paramount object in this struggle is to save the Union and it is not either to save or to destroy slavery. If I could save the Union without freeing any slaves, I would do it; and if I could save it by freeing all the slaves I would do it; and if I could save it by freeing some slaves and leaving others alone I would do that.

"What I do about slavery and the colored race I do because I believe it helps to save the Union ... I shall do less whenever I believe that what I am doing hurts the cause, and I shall do more whenever I believe doing more helps the cause." (Johnson, 468, 469: different texts circulated, 1012n84).

Barkan (287) adds: "The antislavery actions of the U.S. were motivated by the political beliefs of the majority, not as an apology" to the slaves. Hence the abolition cannot be said to have constituted atonement or apology. (By analogy, the defeat of Nazism was a necessary precondition but did not constitute reparation).

Chapter 3 - **Three Biblical Lessons**

1. A black man at the airport needed one more dollar to purchase his ticket to Africa. He approached a white man standing nearby, and told him of his plight. The white man replied, "Here's five dollars, take four more with you!"
2. Leviticus 19.13; Deuteronomy 24.14-15; cf. Job 24.10; Jeremiah 22.13; Malachi 3.5.
3. Matthew 10.10; Luke 10.7; 1 Timothy 5.18.
4. It amazes me that attorney Rotan E. Lee has so much to say about contracts in his article, "Reparations will give us our 'forty acres'," *The Philadelphia Tribune,* 22 June 2001, 7A. Black slavery in America was not a contractual matter. There was no written agreement between owner and slave. So all of Lee's words about a contractual obligation to pay reparation are null and void.

Chapter 4 - **The Jews, the Holocaust and Black Slavery**

1. Korn, 13,16; Thomas, 12, 270-271, 299, 743.
2. Banks, *The Bible and Black Slavery in the U.S.,* chapter 3, pp 24-30.
3. In the 1850 census, 51 Jewish Charlestonians, of the 500 Jews who lived there, owned 288 slaves. Of the 3,441 free blacks in Charleston, 266 of them owned 1,087 slaves: Rosen, 382n23.
4. Christian Science Monitor, 12 Jan 2001, p 2; *The Philadelphia Inquirer,* 31 May 2001, pA9.
5. Cf. "The Lesson of German Redress," Schuchter, Appendix C, 240-244.
6. Tony Czuczka, *The Philadelphia Inquirer,* 7 May 2001. Cf. Daniel Jonah Goldhagen's *Hitler's Willing Executioners: Ordinary Germans and the Holocaust.* The author contends that the German people acted "as they did because of a widespread, profound, unquestioned, and virulent anti-Semitism that led them

to regard the Jews as a demonic enemy whose extermination was not only necessary but also just."

7. Lecky and Wright, 19; concerning dislike for the Jews, see Malcolm X, *Autobiography* 372-373.

8. Munford (415) is unaware of the facts concerning Jewish suffering. He states: "Now if the white world can compensate white Jewry, it should compensate Blacks for our much greater losses over a much longer span of time."

9. During the early days of Reconstruction the blacks were of less value. They were on their "own" since they were no longer "owned." The level of mistreatment was raised a notch, and the life of the freedman became of even less value in the eyes of certain whites.

Chapter 5 - **The Amount and How Spent**

1. "Where planters had fled, abandoning their properties, the freed slaves had in numerous instances seized control and they gave little indication after the war of yielding their authority to the returning owners ... seizures revealed the intensity of black feelings about the land ... " (Litwack, 400). I highly recommend reading ***The Forty Acres Documents,*** published by The Malcolm Generation, Inc., PO Box 74080, Baton Rouge, LA, 70874.

2. Josephus Daniels (*Tar Heel Editor*, 1939, pp 171-172) tells this story: "When I was eighteen I recall asking an old Confederate, 'What was so bad about the promise to give every Negro head of a family forty acres and a mule? Wouldn't that have been better than to turn the ignorant ex-slave without a dollar over to the mercy of Republican politicians, white and black, who made political slaves of them? And if each Negro had been given a piece of land, for which Uncle Sam would pay the Southern owner, wouldn't it have been better for the white man and the Negro?'

"The old man looked at me as if I were a curious individual to be raising such an unheard-of question. 'No,' he said emphatically, 'for it would have made the Negro "uppity," and besides, they don't know enough to farm without direction, and smart white men and Negroes would have gotten the land away from them, and they'd have been worse off than ever ...The real reason,' pursued the old man, 'why it wouldn't do, is that we are having a hard time now keeping the n----- in his place, and if he were a landowner he'd think he was a bigger man than old Grant, and there would be no living with him in the Black district ... Who'd work the land if the n------- had farms of their own ...?'" (Myrdahl, 226-227).

Chapter 6 - **Who Pays and Who Receives?**

1. "Some African Americans are descended from persons who came to the U.S. long after slavery was abolished, including the thousands of Haitians, Dominicans, and other Caribbean immigrants of the last 30 years. These persons' ancestors may have been slaves in their native land, but should the U.S. have to pay for the sins of all slaveowning nations?" Linda Chavez, "The Solution: To treat others as true equals," *The Philadelphia Inquirer,* Sunday, 27 May 2001, A E5).

2. Jack Poinsett, *Ebony Magazine,* August 1965, "Poverty Amidst Plenty," 104-112.

3. I am sure Munford would label me a neo-conservative. He includes in this "accommodationists" list: Charles Barkley, Alan Keyes, Thomas Sowell, Glen Loury, David E. McClean, Roy Innis, Shelby Steele, Stanley Crouch, Stephen Carter, and Colin Powell. Judge Clarence Thomas is especially lambasted. And Booker T. Washington is accused of following a "capitulationist

strategy" (Munford, 311-320).
4. Graham, L.O., *USN & WR*, 15 Feb 1999, 49.

Chapter 7 - **Humanism**

1. To further complicate matters, there is the political aspect of reparation. You will note that I have said nothing of significance relating to the political side of the reparation controversy. The political is tied in with the legal. Reed (17) claims it is incomprehensible that the reparation movement should disregard the question, "How can we imagine building a political force that would enable us to prevail on this issue?"

2. I must admit I have never read a book that spelled out the racist evils perpetrated against black Americans the way Munford tells it. His work is enlightening, depressing, and maddening. If any whites think they have a strong stomach for descriptions of white racism, I recommend reading, *Race and Reparations: A Black Perspective for the 21st Century,* Clarence J. Munford, Africa World Press, Inc., Trenton, NJ, 1996.

Chapter 8 - **Heritability**

1. Whatever persecution these whites initially suffered was short-lived. Because of their white skin they were all the more rapidly assimilated into mainstream society. As for fighting as a Union soldier in the Civil War, how do we know their main objective was to end slavery? We do not.

BIBLIOGRAPHY and REFERENCES

America, Richard F. *Paying the Social Debt.* Praeger Publishers, Westport, Conn., 1993.
American Heritage Dictionary, The. Houghton Mifflin Co., Boston, 1992, third edition.
Anderson, S.E. *Holocaust for Beginners.* Writers & Readers Publishing, Inc. NY, 1995.
Banks, Wm. L. *The Bible and Black Slavery in the U.S.* Infinity Publishing Co., Haverford, Pa. 1999.
_____. *The Black Church in the U.S.* Infinity, 2001.
Barkan, Elazar. *The Guilt of Nations.* WW Norton, NY, 2000.
Barnes, Albert. *Psalms,* vol 3, Baker, G.R., Mich.: 1973.
_____. *An Inquiry into the Scriptural Views of Slavery.* Detroit: Negro History Press, 1969.
Barnett, Victoria. *Christian Century.*"Payback? Racism, Reparation and Accountability." 25 Oct 2000, 1070-1073.
Bennett, Lerone. *The Shaping of Black America.* Johnson Publishing Co., Chicago, 1975.
Berlin, Ira. *Many Thousands Gone.* Belknap Press, Harvard University Press, Cambridge, Mass., 1998.
Bittker, Boris I. *The Case for Black Reparations.* Random House, NY, 1973.
Brown, F; Driver, S.R.; Briggs, C.A. *A Hebrew and English Lexicon of the Old Testament.* Oxford: Clarendon Press, 1952.
Browne, Robert S. *Review of Black Political Economy, The.* Winter, 1993, v21, n 3, 99 (12). "The Economic Basis for Reparations to Black America."
Cone, James H. and Wilmore, Gayraud S. *Black Theology: A Documentary History,* vol 1, 1966-1979. Orbis Books, 1993.
Curtin, Philip. *The Atlantic Slave Trade.* University of Wisconsin Press, Madison, 1969.

Czuczka, Tony. *The Philadelphia Inquirer,* 7 May 01.
Davidson, Basil. *The African Slave Trade.* Little, Brown & Co., Boston, 1961.
D'Souza, Dinesh. *The End of Racism.* The Free Press, NY, 1995.
Du Bois, W.E.B., *Black Reconstruction in America, 1860 - 1880.* August Meier, gen.ed. Atheneum, N.Y., 1985.
Ebony Magazine, August 1965, 1969, 1970.
Encyclopaedia Britannica CD - Dictionary, 1998 Standard Edition
English, E. Schuyler, ed. *The Pilgrim Study Bible.* Oxford University Press, NY. 1976.
Faber, Eli. *Jews, Slaves, and the Slave Trade.* NY University Press, NY, 1998.
Graham, Lawrence O. "Living in a Class Apart." *U.S. News & World Report,* 15 Feb 1999, 49.
Harper's Magazine, Nov, 2000: Forum, 37-51: "Making the Case for Racial Reparations -- Does American Owe a Debt to the Descendants of Its Slaves?"
Haselden, Kyle. *The Racial Problem in Christian Perspective.* Harper & Bros., NY, 1959.
Herf, Jeffrey. *Divided Memory: The Nazi Past in the Two Germanys.* Harvard University Press, Cambridge, Mass., 1997
Horowitz, David. "Ten Reasons Why Reparations for Slavery Is a Bad Idea." *FrontpageMagazine.com,* 3 Jan 2001.
Hughes, Graham. "Reparations for Blacks?", NY University Law Review, 43 (Dec 1968), 1063-74.
Hurston, Zora Neale. *Dust Tracks on a Road.* GK Hall & Co. Thorndike, Maine, 1997 (large print ed.)
Jackson, Basil. "Psychology, Psychiatry, and the Pastor," part IV. The Spiritual Dimensions of Drug Abuse, *Bibliotheca Sacra,* vol 132, #528, Oct 1975.
Johnson, Paul. *A History of the American People.* HarperCollins Publishers, NY, 1997.

Kalisher, Meno. *Israel My Glory.* May/June 2001, 29.
Keil, C.F. & Delitzsch, F. *Commentary on the Old Testament,* vol 1, Pentateuch; vol 5, Psalms. Eerdmans, G.R., Mich., 1980.
Kirkpatrick, A.F. ed. *The Book of Psalms.* Cambridge University Press, London, 1903.
Krauthammer, Charles. *The Philadelphia Inquirer,* 9 Apr 2001; *Time Magazine,* 31 Dec 1990, 18.
Kunjufu, Jawanza. *Black Economics.* African American Images, Chicago, 1991.
Lecky, Robert S. and Wright, H. Elliott, eds. *Black Manifesto: Religion, Racism & Reparation.* Sheed & Ward, NY: 1969.
Lenski, R.C.H. *The Interpretation of the Epistle to the Hebrews and the Epistle of James.* Augsburg Publishing House, Minneapolis, Minn. 1961.
Leupold, H.C. *Exposition of Psalms.* Baker Book House, G.R. Mich., 1972.
Lincoln, C. Eric & Mamiya, Lawrence H. *The Black Church in the African American Experience.* Duke University Press, Durham, NC, 1991, second impression.
Litwack, Leon F. *North of Slavery: The Negro in the Free States 1790 - 1860.* University of Chicago Press, Chicago,1970.
Lockerbie, D. Bruce. "Thinking Like a Christian," part 3, A Call for Christian Humanism, *Bibliotheca Sacra,* vol 143, #571, July 1986. Dallas, Texas.
Magnet, Myron. *The Dream and the Nightmare.* Quill William Morrow, NY, 1993.
Malcolm X. (As told to Alex Haley). *Autobiography.* Ballantine Books, NY, 1965.
Marketti, Jim. "Black Equity in the Slave Industry," Review of Black Political Economy, 2:2 (1972), 43-66.
Mercer, Larry A. "A Biblical and Cultural Study of the Problem of Racism." *Bibliotheca Sacra* 153 (Jan-Mar 1966), 93. Dallas.
Muhammad, Elijah. *Message to the Blackman in America.*

Muhammad Mosque of Islam #2, Chicago, 1965.
Munford, Clarence J. *Race and Reparations: A Black Perspective for the 21st Century.* Africa World Press, Inc. Trenton, NJ. 1996.
National Coalition of Blacks for Reparations (N'COBRA), Washington, D.C.
Nelson Study Bible, The (NKJV). Earl D. Radmacher, gen ed, Nelson Publishers, Nashville, 1997.
Newsweek Mazagine, 30 June 1969, 31.
Philadelphia Inquirer, The. 13 Jan 1970; 7 Jan 1992; 27 Mar; 9 Apr; 7, 20, 27, 28, 31 May 2001.
Philadelphia Tribune, The. 27 Feb; 7 Mar; 10, 13, 22, 24, 27 Apr; 29 May 01.
Plummer, Alfred. *A Critical and Exegetical Commentary: Gospel According to S. Luke (ICC).* T. & T. Clark: Edinburgh, 1969.
Poinsett, Alex, "Poverty Amidst Plenty," *Ebony Magazine,* August 1965, 104-112.
Proctor, Samuel DeWitte. *The Substance of Things Hoped For.* G.P. Putnam's Sons, NY. 1995.
Random House Unabridged Dictionary, CD-Rom, 1993.
Reed, Adolph L. Jr. "The Case Against Reparations," *The Progressive,* Dec 2000, 15-17.
Robinson, Randall. *The Debt: What America Owes to Blacks.* Plume -Penquin Group, NY, 2001.
Ropes, James H. *Epistle of James.* Edinburgh: T & T Clark, 1973.
Rosen, Robert N. *The Jewish Confederates.* University of South Carolina Press, Columbia, SC, 2000.
Rustin, Bayard. "The Myths of the Black Revolt." *Ebony Magazine,* Aug 1969, 96-104.
Schuchter, Arnold. *Reparations--The Black Manifesto and Its Challenge to White America.* JB Lippincott Co. Phila., 1970.
Sider, Ronald J. "Corporate Guilt, Institutional Racism & Holiness." Seminar; Christian Holiness Association,

Louisville, KY, April 18-19, 1974.
Sowell, Thomas. *Race and Culture: A World View.* Basic Books, Perseus Books Group, NY, 1994.
Speare, M. Edmund, ed. *The Pocket Book of Verse.* Pocket Books Inc., NY 1944.
Spurgeon, C.H. *The Treasury of David.* Vol 2. MacDonald Publishing Co., McLean, Va., n.d.
Tadman, Michael. *Speculators and Slaves.* The University of Wisconsin Press, Madison, Wisconsin, 1996.
Thayer, Joseph H. *Greek-English Lexicon of the New Testament.* G.R., Mich.: Zondervan, 1965.
Thernstrom, S. & Thernstrom, Abigail. *America in Black and White: One Nation, Indivisible.* Simon & Shuster, NY, 1997.
Thomas, Hugh. *The Slave Trade: The Story of the Atlantic Slave Trade: 1440-1870.* Simon & Shuster, NY. 1997.
Thornton, John Kelly. *Africa and Africans in the Making of the Atlantic World, 1400-1680.* Cambridge University Press, 1998.
Wachtel, Paul L. *Race in the Mind of America.* Routledge, NY, 1999.
Washington, Linn. *The Philadelphia Tribune, 24 April, 2001.* "Media to Blame for Lack of Reparations," 29 May 2001, 7A.
White, Jack E. "Don't Waste Your Breath," *Time Magazine,* 2 Apr 2001, 48.
Woodson, Carter G. ed. *Free Negro Owners of Slaves in the United States in 1830.* Negro Universities Press, Westport, Conn., second printing, 1973.
World Book Dictionary, The. Barnhart, C.L. & Barnhart, R.K., eds. 2 vols. World Book, Inc.: Chicago, 1983.
Worrill, Conrad W. *The Philadelphia Tribune,* 7 Mar; 24 Apr 2001.
Zodhiates, Spiros. *The Behavior of Belief.* Eerdmans, G.R. 1966.

INDEX

Abolitionists, 24, 47, 65, 67
Affirmative Action, 5f, 34, 39, 53, 59f
Africans selling Africans, 43-45
America, Richard, 35, 57
American Colonization Society, 21
American Indians, see Native Americans, 11, 46, 52, 75
Anderson, S.E., 23
Anti-Semitism, 25-28, 30f, 98
Barkan, Elazar, 29, 35, 47, 96f
Berlin, Ira, 61
Bitterness, 63, 67, 76
Bittker, Boris, 38, 57
Black Manifesto, 7f, 13, 35, 77-90
Black Muslims, 23
Blacks who owned slaves, 49
Brock, Robert, 35
Chavez, Linda, 6, 100
Colonialists in Africa, 45
"Comfort women," 11
Conyers, John Jr., 9, 13, 37
Davis, David Brion, 23
Diaspora, The, 26
Du Bois, W.E.B., 42
Emancipation Proclamation, 2f, 13, 32, 41, 49, 65, 94
Exodus, The, 14-17, 19, 75
Farrakhan, Louis, 23f
Forman, James, 7, 35, 84, 88

"Forty acres and a mule," 16, 40-42, 74, 98f
Franklin, John Hope, 66
Free blacks, 1, 17f, 24, 49, 51f, 92, 98
Garvey, Marcus, 16, 37

Greely, Horace, 97
Henly, Wm. Ernest, 54
Holocaust, The, 10, 13, 23, 25-31, 92, 96,98
Horowitz, David, 12f, 47, 66, 91f, 96
Humanism, 53-58, 60, 64, 75
Hurston, Zora Neale, 44
Hutchinson, Earl Ofari, 96
Inquirer, The Philadelphia, 6, 8, 29, 57f, 96, 98, 100
"Invictus," 54
Islam, 48f, 75; see Muslims also
Jackson, Dr. J. H., 7
Japanese-Americans, 3, 10f, 92
Jews, 10, 14f, 22-27, 29-31, 68, 70, 74f, 77, 86, 88, 92, 98f
Johnson, Andrew, 41
Kenyatta, Muhammad, 8f, 88
King, Martin Luther, Jr., 13, 55
Krauthammer, Charles, 34, 55
Kunjufu, J., 34.46
Lee, Rotan E., 98
Legal, legalism, 41, 51, 56-58, 101
Lincoln, Abraham, 13, 97
Loury, Glen, 6, 100
Madhubuti, Haki, 35
Magnet, Myron, 63
Malcolm X, 38, 55, 70, 99
Marketti, Jim, 34
McGriff, Milton, 3
Mouson, Geir, 29

Muhammad, Elijah, 16, 37f
Munford, Clarence J., 50, 55, 60, 63, 96, 99, 101
Muslims, The, 44, 47f ; Black Muslims, 23
Myers, John, 57
Myrdahl, Gunnar, 42, 51
Nazis, The, 10, 25, 27-30, 97
N'COBRA (National Coalition of Blacks
 for Reparation in America), 35, 58, 96
Nation of Islam, 23f
Native Americans, 11, 46, 52, 75
Nisei, 10, 13
"Passing", 51
Paternalism, 6, 8, 36, 74
Poinsett, Alex, 100
Population: Slaves, 1, 17
Poverty, 2, 32-34, 39, 46, 64
Proctor, Dr. Samuel DeWitte, 37, 59, 66
Reconciliation, 1, 6, 58
Reconstruction, 12, 41, 99
"Reconstructionists", 53
Relocation of blacks, 37f
Reparation: defined, 2-4; growth of movement, 9f;
 renewed interest, 5-7
Reparations: defined, 3f ; examples, 10f
Republic of New Africa, 34, 37
Rich oppressors, 20f
Rivera, Elaine, 59
Robinson, Randall, 12f, 30, 32, 47, 55, 58-60, 70, 92
Rosewood, Fla., 11, 92, 96
Rustin, Bayard, 7, 47
Sabaoth, Lord of , 20-22
Self-esteem, 2, 60-63
Sharpton, Rev. Alfred, 35

Sherman, William, 40f
Sherrod, L.G., 41
Sider, Dr. Ron, 68
Slave Trade: numbers, 1, 48
Sowell, Thomas, 36, 40, 48, 63, 70, 100

Stevens, Thaddeus, 41
Swanson, Lillian, 58
Swinton, David, 35
Thomas, Hugh, 23
Thornton, John Kelly, 45
Tribune, The Philadelphia, 3, 64, 66, 98
Tulsa, Okla., 11
Tuskegee, 11, 92
Underground Railroad, The, 47, 65
Union soldiers, 13, 40, 46f, 52, 65, 91, 101
Universal Negro Improvement Association, 37
Wealthy black Americans, 46f
Welfare, 2, 5, 35, 63, 80, 84f, 94
White, Jack E., 34
Worrill, Conrad W., 2, 63, 66
Zacchaeus, 17-20, 22, 75

William L. Banks

Northeast High School - 1945
University of Pennsylvania - BA, 1953
Lincoln Seminary - BD, 1957
Carver Bible College - DD, 1973
Eastern Baptist Theological Seminary - M Th, 1959; D Min, 1982

Made in the USA
Monee, IL
28 April 2026

49136500R00069